If You Like My Apples

A Simple Guide to Biodynamic Gardening

If You Like My Apples

A Simple Guide to Biodynamic Gardening

Clue Tyler Dennis
Luke Miller

Avery Publishing Group

Garden City Park, New York

Text Illustrator: John Wincek
Cover Art: Bryan Haynes
Cover Design: William Gonzalez and Rudy Shur
In-House Editor: Linda Stern
Contributing Editor: Janet Lively

Library of Congress Cataloging-in Publication Data
Dennis, Clue Tyler
    If you like my apples: a simple guide to biodynamic gardening /
    Clue Tyler Dennis, Luke Miller.
        p. cm.
    Includes bibliographical references and index.
    ISBN 0-89529-760-4 (pbk.)
    1. Organic gardening. I. Miller, Luke. II. Title.
    SB453.5.D46 1997
    635'.0484—dc21   96-46976
                                                      CIP

Printed in the United States of America

10 9 8 7 6 5 4 3 2 1

Contents

Acknowledgements

I would like to thank my fellow naturalists Janet Lively and Luke Miller, who not only contributed parts of this book, but to whom I am indebted for their friendship and support.

—C.T.D.

Preface

This book was written to be earth friendly. We believe that all gardening is a dialogue between soul and soil, and that gardeners are mediators, artists who listen to what plants and the environment have to tell us.

The essentials of biodynamic gardening are simply those of applied ecology, which is central to the search for an alternative to the use of chemicals in the garden. Agricultural experiment stations across the country are now studying the biodynamic method in an effort to avoid the depletion of the nutrients in both soil and environment.

While most gardeners practice a certain amount of natural rotating, composting, and care of the soil, many fall victim to the advertised promises of great returns and protection to be gotten from the use of chemicals. We are told that the air and soil are overrun with insect infestations and that to survive we must arm ourselves with sprays. Nothing is said about destroying the delicate balance in air and soil.

This book attempts to provide real help to those who seek a sane, safe, and ecologically sound method of gardening.

1

What Is the Biodynamic Movement?

*The return of sensible farming
and gardening practices*

Organic farming is now on the official agenda of everything agricultural. To the surprise of many, the U.S. Department of Agriculture has endorsed many organic farming techniques and has recommended development of educational programs and informational materials to help county extension agents serve organic farmers. Help of this order will reduce dependence on energy, stem the decline of soil productivity, alleviate environmental degradation, and strengthen family farms and localized marketing systems.

THE DEMAND FOR CHEMICAL-FREE FARMING

The nearly 600 chemicals that farmers use to kill insects and weeds are coming under growing public and governmental scrutiny, feared as soil and water contaminants and blamed for causing cancer. Their effectiveness is also in question. Insects have developed immunity to many agricultural pesticides, and scientists at Cornell University have established that some chemicals interfere with a plant's ability to withstand weather conditions. A plant sprayed with an insecticide may be able to ward off caterpillars but end up dying in a hailstorm.

Farming without chemicals, once considered an impractical and idealistic fringe movement, is moving closer to the mainstream of agriculture in the United States. Major growers in Iowa now plant rye after the corn harvest. During the winter, the decomposing rye produces natural weed-killing substances that protect the fields in the spring and make the use of chemical herbicides unnecessary. In California, some farmers plant catnip between rows of vegetables to drive away destructive insects.

Even skeptics in the agricultural community admit that alternatives to chemical technology must be found, since the chemical method of farming not only costs billions of dollars each year, it also threatens environmental contamination and the eventual destruction of the soil. But condemnation of chemical technology is coming from an even more powerful group: the public. The consequences of the use of chemicals in the food we eat have moved consumers toward a more demanding stance. Food markets now readily display signs announcing organically grown products.

The government has been slow to recognize the health dangers and environmental risks posed by agricultural chemicals. Its policy has been to encourage farmers to get as many bushels per acre as conceivably possible. Now, public concern is encouraging both government and the agricultural community to consider using the dynamic biological interrelationships in nature to achieve the same results as chemical pesticides and fertilizers. While the overriding purpose behind organic farming is to maintain the purity and availability of renewable resources such as water and soil, growers who correctly employ its principles should also see production costs drop and profits rise.

In essence, there is a return of some of the age-old farming practices that lost favor when pesticides and fertilizers became widely available. New techniques have been developed through research and careful experimenting. Now, instead of turning to spray guns at the first sight of a weed or an insect, farmers and scientists are beginning to reach a better understanding of the complex interactions in nature. Key to this understanding is an awareness of the life of the soil. Soil is an integrated system that includes all life—a subterranean world of microscopic forces and biological activities. To comprehend it, we must prepare to see the unseen.

THE ORIGINS OF BIODYNAMICS

Organic farming is a method of cultivation that excludes the use of synthetically compounded fertilizers, pesticides, growth regulators, and livestock feed additives. Instead, organic legumes, green manures, mechanical cultivation, mineral-bearing rocks, and biological pest control are used to maintain soil productivity. Biodynamics embraces many of the same techniques as organic farming; however, it goes beyond the simple implementation of a set of techniques.

In defining biodynamics, we must start with the theorist of the movement, European philosopher Dr. Rudolf Steiner, and his philosophy of anthroposophy, developed around the turn of the century. Dr. Steiner's speculations on the spiritual nature of man led him to the belief that the earth is a living organism with its own life rhythms and complex system of relationships, including the influence of sun, moon, stars, and planets. Following this belief, the biodynamic gardener does not force alien patterns on the land but works with nature, stimulating the soil and the plants to fulfill their potential. In biodynamics, correct timing of operations is as important as the proper balance of conditions on the land.

Biodynamic farming sees a farm as a self-supporting system. Livestock feed off the land and provide manure. Composted vegetation and manure fertilize the land, returning nutrients to it. Finally, the land grows new vegetation for consumption. It is the goal of the biodynamic farmer to know what each plant needs to grow well. Growing healthful produce in a natural, self-sustaining environment, rather than producing spectacular yields, is the aim. Dr. Steiner emphasized that biodynamics is a state of mind as much as a set of techniques.

Another pioneer in this field was Dr. Ehrenfried Pfeiffer, who made biodynamic teaching his life work. A disciple of Dr. Steiner's, Dr. Pfeiffer served as the director of the Biochemical Research Laboratory at the Goetheanum Dornach, Switzerland. His teaching influenced the educational trust that established classes in the biodynamics in the curriculum at Pierce Agricultural College in California.

BIODYNAMICS IN THE GARDEN

Biodynamic ideas are not essentially new. Our ancestors practiced biodynamic gardening simply by not putting foreign materials into the soil or onto plants. They worked the soil by growing certain plants near other plants, a technique that scientists are now beginning to rediscover. Studies have established beyond any doubt that trace elements and minerals—nature's own hormones—work much better without interference from synthetic products.

In the following chapters, we will explain how soil, weather, and topography affect vegetation, and suggest ways to adapt your garden, lawn, or woodlot to the conditions of your land. Tips on compost, fertilizer, companion planting, natural pesticides, and weeds will further help you capitalize on nature's inherent synergism.

While these biodynamic techniques apply to commercial farms, our focus is on private gardens, whether they're located on a small acreage or a city lot. We hope to provide a mix of theory and practical application that will be useful to both experienced and novice gardeners. This is an invitation to look at your land from earthworm level and to garden in sync with nature's rhythms.

2

Understanding Conditions: The Key to Planning

*Careful planning for a better garden
with less fuss*

While there are many ways to help plants thrive, gardeners can't do much to change the topography of their land, the weather, or the appetite of neighborhood wildlife. By studying these conditions, however, you can make the necessary adaptations in your garden plan. And you will want to have a detailed plan written out well before planting time. Biodynamic gardening is a complicated puzzle with too many pieces to keep only in your head.

SURVEYING YOUR LAND

One of the first steps in planning a garden is to survey your land. Take a shovel so you can examine the soil in different parts of the property. The texture and condition of the soil affect your garden in many ways, which are discussed in a separate chapter. (See Chapter 4 for details.) Try to find a garden spot away from trees and buildings; naturally, a garden should be in a clearing that provides maximum sun. But it should not be near a highway. Carbon monoxide does not improve the growth of your plants.

Scout for puddles and soggy areas, which are signs of poor drainage. Good drainage is of paramount importance in the garden, so important that drainage measures take priority over compost and fertilizer. Topography influences drainage, as does the texture of the soil. One of the best ways to guarantee a well-drained garden is to put it in a sloping area. Barring this, you can ensure good drainage by using ditches, aerating soil to a depth of a foot or more, adding green manure, and using proper planting techniques.

You don't need perfectly flat land for a garden, but hills and hollows require their own style of farming. It takes a special kind of person to make a success of growing crops on

Figure 2.1. A Terraced Garden.

a steep hillside. Hillside gardeners have to be well-tuned to the many subtleties of soil permeability and groundwater movement, wind exposure, and the severity of slope. Every hillside farm possesses a texture and character all its own. With its need for fallow periods, long-range rotations, grass ways, and diversion terraces, hilly land often cannot be farmed as intensively as flat land. The back terraces and slopes are too steep for conventional crops but ideally suited to specialty crops like berries and grapes.

Erosion is a problem in hillside gardens, but it can be controlled with contour farming techniques. Instead of laying garden beds in solid rectangles or squares, plant crops in strips that follow the contour of the hills at right angles to the slopes. (See Figure 2.1 for an idea of how this is done.) Plant grass or hay in between these strips. Steeper slopes require

more abrupt terraces, which can be quite steep on the back or downslope side. The backside is not cultivated but kept permanently in grass terraces. Terraces slow and even halt the downward flow of run-off water. The low areas between rolling hills, where large volumes of water flow during rainstorms, should be kept in grass sod. If not sodded, such areas soon erode into unproductive gullies.

UNDERSTANDING YOUR CLIMATE

Once you are familiar with the lay of your land, you'll need to research the climate. Find out the average rainfall for your area, as well as the average summer temperature and the dates of the last frost in the spring and the first frost in the fall. The source of such data should be as local as possible, since lakes and hills can create microclimates. Even the type of soil on your land will affect the temperature of the air and the garden bed. Air warms up more slowly over a heavy clay soil than over rocky, sandy soils. Sandy areas cool off faster than wooded areas.

Drought may be inevitable in your area, but by planning for it, you can help your vegetables survive. First, mulch to conserve water. A mulch is anything that conserves the moisture in the soil by reducing the rate of evaporation. Mulch also greatly reduces the presence of weeds, which is important because weeds compete with vegetable crops for every drop of water. The stronger, deeper-rooted weeds often win the competition.

Many organic materials may be used as mulches, as explained in Chapter 8. Plastic mulch, available in many garden centers, also works and is reusable for several seasons. Put down mulch when the soil is moist, even if you're not ready to plant. You can push back the mulch at planting time or cut slits or holes in the plastic.

Another tip for drought control is to take advantage of shade. Moisture evaporates more slowly in shaded soil. Leafy vegetables such as cabbage, lettuce, spinach, and Swiss chard do well in partial shade—areas that receive full sun for only part of the day. Basil, mint, parsley, and tarragon are a few herbs that also thrive in partial shade. Fruiting vegetables such as tomatoes, peppers, and vine crops need full sun.

Groundwater evaporates more slowly in areas where rainfall is heaviest in spring and fall. Take advantage of spring and fall growing seasons by planting vegetables that like cool conditions, such as beets, broccoli, cabbage, cauliflower, collards, kale, kohlrabi, lettuce, mustard greens, onions, peas, spinach, Swiss chard, and turnips. Plant these crops early so they finish production before the hot summer. Or sow them in summer as recommended on seed packets, but keep the seed bed constantly moist for good germination. They'll be established in fall and thrive in the cooler weather.

Summer crops, such as tomatoes, soybeans, cucumbers, and squash, should be planted earlier in drought areas to encourage bearing before the hot days arrive. If unusually late spring frost threatens, cover the young plants at night with commercially available hot caps, made out of waxed paper; inverted plastic milk jugs; or other protective devices. Remove such covers in the morning.

For more shade protection, space plants and rows so the mature plants just overlap. This will help reduce the moisture loss and weed competition. However, the narrow rows will make it difficult to use a mechanical cultivator. Regular harvesting also reduces the moisture requirements of the plants and encourages continued production. Pick when they are at their prime; don't let them become overripe.

Water in the evening and early morning. You can use special soil-soaking hoses, which allow water to drip slowly into the ground. Place these hoses quite close to the plants. You can also set your garden hose, nozzle removed, directly on the ground to irrigate one part of your garden at a time. A deep soaking is needed only every 10 to 14 days, unless your plants show signs of wilting from insufficient moisture. Remember that oscillating lawn sprinklers allow for much more evaporation than other watering methods.

You can save water, literally, by keeping two covered barrels or spare trash cans near the house or garden to hold recycled water. If possible, reroute your roof gutters and downspouts into the barrels.

PROTECTING AGAINST WILDLIFE

In addition to covering weather and topography, your garden plan needs to provide protection from visiting animals. For example, a wall of onions will keep out rabbits. Raccoons don't like vine crops because they stand to eat and their feet get tangled in squash, pumpkins, and cucumbers. Indians planted vine crops between rows of corn, which is a favorite of raccoons. Deer can be easily deterred from the garden by a good planting of wormwood. This spreads rapidly, so be forewarned, but it is better than having your crop eaten by deer.

Varmints can also be deterred with nonpoisonous additives. Rabbits will not nibble carrot stems sprinkled with red pepper after a rain. You can encourage groundhogs to move on by breaking up the soil around their holes and sprinkling it with lime or bonemeal. Garlic offends groundhogs as well. For additional protective techniques against wildlife, see Table 2.1.

Strategic arrangement of crops can also keep away insects and otherwise improve the health of plants. **Companion planting,** as it's called, is basic to organic gardening and is discussed in Chapter 5. It saves time, maintenance, and garden space and should figure prominently in your garden plans.

Table 2.1 Techniques for Dealing With Wildlife

Wildlife	Protective Technique
Deer	Plant wormwood every 2 feet or between crop rows.
Gophers	Plant daffodils.
Mice, moles, and voles	Sprinkle lime around plants. (This is also good for the soil.)
Rabbits	Spread bonemeal, or plant onions. (Rabbits will not pass through onions.)
Raccoons	Plant vine vegetables between corn rows.
Woodchucks	Spread ground pepper, blood meal, or talcum powder.

PLANNING YOUR GARDEN

Once you have gathered information on the topography, climate, and wildlife affecting your garden, you can begin to plan. Planning carefully will give you maximum productiveness, and your garden will require minimum maintenance.

Location

Make sure the garden is conveniently located and accessible to work in. Crowded and crisscrossed rows make work twice as hard. Break a field into squares with paths in between. A large plowed mass is difficult to cultivate, maintain, and harvest.

Key Questions About Your Garden

Ask yourself these questions to see how well you understand your growing environment.

TOPOGRAPHY

- *Is the area sunny? shady? partially shady?*
- *Is the ground level? sloping?*
- *Are there puddles or other signs of poor drainage?*

CLIMATE

- *What are the dates of the first and last frosts? How cold and how hot does it get?*
- *How many inches of rainfall are usual?*
- *When is it the rainiest?*

WILDLIFE

- *Which animals are prevalent?*

Also remember not to plant more than you need or more than you have room to store after harvesting.

Layout

Make diagrams of your garden beds before planting time, outlining which crops go where and when you'll plant them. (See Figures 2.2 and 2.3 for sample garden layouts.)

Seed catalogs give information about the growing seasons of different vegetables and herbs. Our companion planting guide (see page 52) will help you decide how your plants should best be arranged.

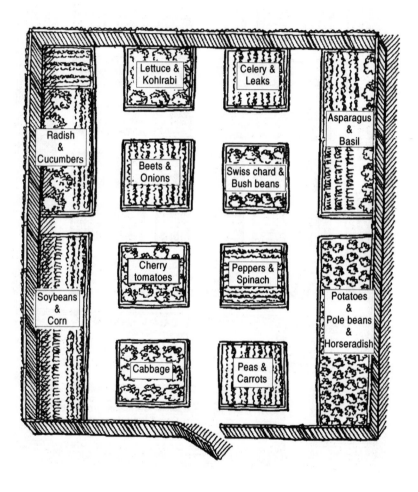

Figure 2.2. Layout for a Small Garden.

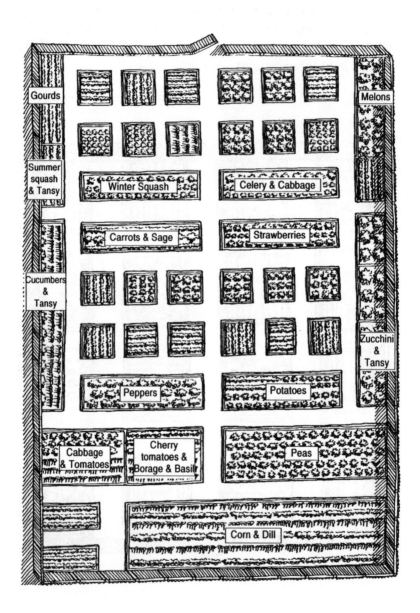

Figure 2.3. Layout for a Large Garden.

Selection

Choose plants that will thrive. Plants are picky about where they live and how much abuse they'll tolerate from humans. You've seen the ill-considered planting of honey-locust trees under utility lines. The trees grow too large and will eventually need to be topped so they don't interfere with the power lines. Similarly, constant bruising from lawn mowers and weed whackers will make trees in your lawn or boulevard ripe for an invasion of insects or disease long before the trees mature. Adding a rim of mulch would protect the trees from battering and save maintenance costs, but that won't change the fact that the wrong trees were used in the first place.

Other examples of poor plant selection include white pines near salted thoroughfares, taxus plants (yews) in water-logged clay soil, Kentucky bluegrass under the heavy shade of a Norway maple, and rhododendrons in sunny, exposed areas. Gardeners can sometimes make do with the wrong plant in the wrong area, but maintenance requires a lot more effort. It's much easier to work with Mother Nature, putting plants in an environment for which they are better suited. Hardy deciduous trees that are more salt-tolerant than evergreens can be used along the highway, while moisture-loving evergreens, such as inkberry, can replace the taxus in wet areas.

Take into consideration how the plant is going to be used. A burning bush makes a great screen, but it grows much too large for small areas. Valerian and yarrow both grow tall and make good borders because they keep out unwanted insects.

Also, pay attention to the Latin, or scientific, names of plants if you know them. Local names can vary. For instance, American elm is called white elm in Canada, but is known as *Ulmus americana* around the globe.

Planting

Use techniques appropriate for the specific plant. Good planting is as important in landscaping as it is in vegetable or herb gardening. The vast majority of **dieback**—a condition in which the peripheral parts of woody plants die in landscape settings—has nothing whatsoever to do with a disease or insect infestation. The latter are merely symptoms of improper placement and incorrect handling. An Austrian pine might fall prey to an attack of pine bark beetles because it was planted too deeply. Conversely, hardy junipers can suffer dieback because their roots were planted too shallow. When planting, make sure the top of the rootball is level with the surrounding ground. If you are dealing with bare-root stock, plant the stem up to its root collar. (See Figure 2.4.) See Chapter 11 for greater detail on planting trees and shrubs.

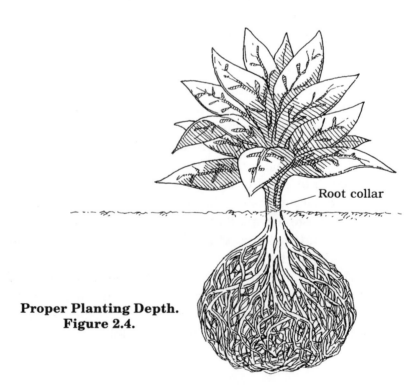

Root collar

Proper Planting Depth.
Figure 2.4.

Records

Keep a year-to-year log of your plantings to help with rotations, and record the success of different varieties and techniques. The log book will help you decide on appropriate combinations of crops and fertilizers.

You can use a plain notebook or a specially designed garden record book. If you are using a notebook, you can rule columns on the pages and add the following headings:

- Date of Planting

- Rainfall Amount (Watering Needed? When?)

- Harvest Date and Quantity

- Ground Tilled after Harvest?

You should also write down observations and thoughts about the garden and the specific plantings. These will help you make decisions in the future.

SOLUTIONS FOR PROBLEM AREAS

You may find that you've got some problem spots in your garden. Here are a few remedies to consider.

Sandy Soil

The easiest thing to plant may be grass, but it will require a good deal of water and fertilizer, since both leach out of sandy soil rather quickly. Why not try a natural-looking landscape that includes rocks surrounded by ornamental grasses and sunflowers? Add in your choice of nasturtium, petunia, portulaca, flowering tobacco, and sweet alyssum.

Adventurers might even try planting so-called weeds, such as dandelion and sedge, but those plants should be confined to a limited area and kept from going to seed. Woody plants such as juniper, black oak, box elder, and mulberry can accent the area, while clover can fill any remaining bare spots.

Soggy Clay Soils

Again, a natural-looking landscape may be your best bet. Plant a grove of silver and red maples, or try ash, aspen, or willow (the latter two are messy, however, and should be used advisedly). Smaller plantings can feature red-twig dogwood, viburnum, ferns, and blue-fig, a beard-less iris.

Shady Areas

Everyone loves myrtle, pachysandra, impatiens, and begonias, but you can also have it made in the shade with periwinkle, hosta, Baltic ivy, lily-of-the-valley, daylily, boxwood, holly, mountain laurel, dogwood, sassafras, serviceberry, hickory, and hornbeam.

Slopes and Banks

Gentle slopes of 20 degrees or less don't usually pose erosion problems, so plant what you like. On steep slopes, it's best to use stem-rooting plants, which are less likely to be washed away or left with exposed roots. By their very nature, slopes are well-drained, so plants that thrive on drier sites are recommended. Try alpine asters, purple rock cress, dwarf bellflower, red valerian, yellow corydalis, rockrose, edelweiss, flower-of-Jove, mountain clematis, yellow or sweet honeysuckle, and Virginia creeper.

Learning about the natural environment that constitutes your growing area—the land, the climate, and the wildlife—is the first step in planning for a garden. Choosing location carefully, laying out the garden in advance, selecting appropriate plants, using good planting techniques, and keeping consistent records will all contribute to a successful and flourishing garden.

3

Useful
Gardening Tools

*Equipment matched
to the job at hand*

Judging by the number of garden catalogs out there, household horticulturists need a huge arsenal of specialized tools before they can do battle in the yard. That simply isn't so.

Many people do very well in the garden using a variety of makeshift and oddball tools—hand-me-downs from grandma, garage-sale rejects, or household utensils pressed into service in a pinch. There's no end to the ingenuity of gardeners. We've been known to use serving spoons as hand trowels and steak knives as weeding implements. Lawn mowers sometimes do double duty as leaf blowers. And scissors work nicely on pliable stems, thank you.

As you start to assemble your tool collection, remember this: Most of these items can be had cheap at garage and estate sales. Some of the other items can be picked up on sale during the off-season. So shop around. After all, the less they cost, the more tools you can buy!

DIGGING

Every gardener has a core collection of tools to rely upon. For digging, you'll need a round-point shovel and a spading fork. A good *round-point shovel* is handy for transplanting, cutting thorny weeds, and slicing sod. A *spading fork*, on the other hand, is valuable for breaking up **hardpan**, a compacted, clayey layer of subsoil that it is nearly impossible for roots to penetrate. It is also useful for digging around rocks and roots, or lifting heavy loads of compacted leaves. And it can be used to remove plants without damaging the roots.

Look for a "solid forged" round-point shovel so there's no bending or giving when the blade strikes hard ground. To save wear on your feet, the shovel should have a thick lip where it comes into contact with your shoe (a narrow lip pinpoints the pressure and is sure to bring pain). With a spading fork, you can get an English-style utensil, with sharp, square tines that pierce soil easily, or a traditional fork with broad, flat tines especially suited for digging in heavier soils.

Three other useful forks are a *pitchfork*, which has five tines and is as well suited to light work, such as spreading or collecting hay; a *composting fork*, which has five shorter and slightly thicker tines, for turning heavy compost; and a *scoop fork*, which has ten tines and serves the same purposes as a standard pitchfork. If budget is a concern, a spading fork can be substituted for any of these tools. Figure 3.1 shows several kinds of digging tools.

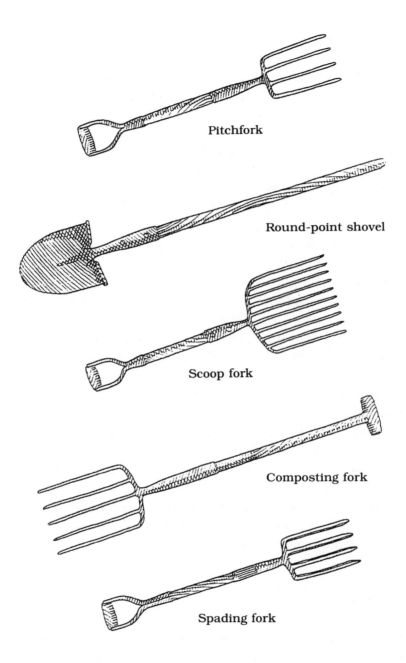

Pitchfork

Round-point shovel

Scoop fork

Composting fork

Spading fork

Figure 3.1. Digging Tools.

CULTIVATING

For general yard raking, there are three popular choices available: spring steel rakes, poly rakes, and bamboo rakes. *Spring steel rakes* are best for heavy-duty raking, when you want to remove thatch or moss, for instance. They're usually available with 18-inch or 22-inch heads. *Poly rakes* and *bamboo rakes* are fine for surface leaf raking. They don't have any metal parts to loosen or rust. And bamboo rakes are available with a 30-inch head, which allows you to cover more ground.

Heavy rakes are a must for anyone planting a vegetable garden or putting in a new lawn, since they're invaluable for roughing up and smoothing soil. A *heavy steel rake* is all the homeowner really needs. They're available with straight or curved teeth, depending on your preference. A *wood grading rake*, especially one with a large spread—say, 28 inches—is handy for big jobs, like putting in a lawn. Golf courses also use them for sand trap maintenance. Fortunately, the typical homeowner doesn't have to worry about that!

For weeding and cultivating, a standard *planter hoe* fits the bill just fine. The nursery catalogs have a slew of different styles for sale. There's a Dutch scuffle hoe, the pointed push hoe, and the weeding hoe, also known as an oscillating hoe. But all you really need is a planter hoe. Use it for trenching, weeding, cultivating, and grading. Figure 3.2 illustrates several kinds of cultivating tools.

CUTTING

In the days before weed whackers, gardeners used funny-looking grass shears on wheels. Although specialty catalogs still have them, the "rolling shears" aren't a staple of

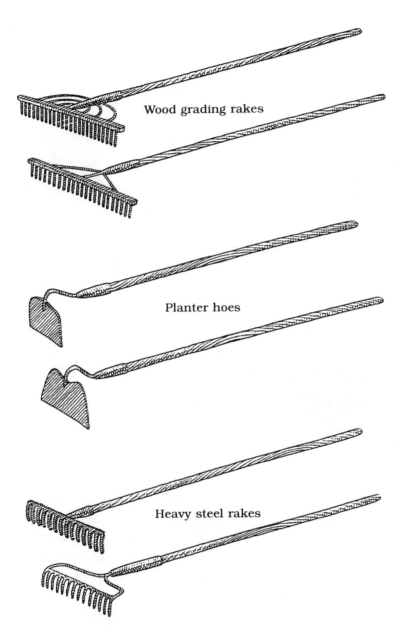

Wood grading rakes

Planter hoes

Heavy steel rakes

Figure 3.2. Cultivating Tools.

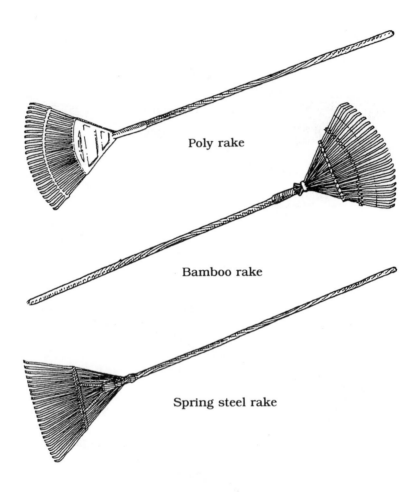

Poly rake

Bamboo rake

Spring steel rake

too many tool sheds anymore. They've been replaced with gas-powered weed whackers and electric edgers.

Well, if you don't mind putting the muscle back in gardening, manual grass shears will do just fine around the house. For durability, you may wish to consider professional-quality drop-forged *grass shears*, or *sheep shears*, which have an offset handle and can be sharpened easily.

For edging, a *rotary edger and trimmer* does the trick nicely. If sod has been neglected for some time, it will take a bit more muscle to edge the lawn the first time. But after that, the rotary edger will glide effortlessly on its rubber wheel, cutting near-perfect lines with a circular blade that revolves with each push and pull.

When it comes to ornamental plants, you'll need four basic tools: hand-held pruner, lopping shears, hedge shears, and saw. The *hand-held pruner* is available in an anvil style, which brings the cutting blade directly down

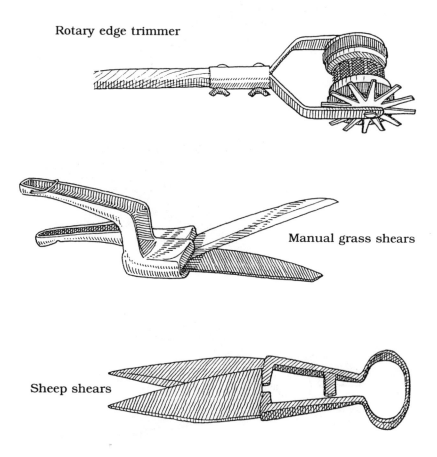

Rotary edge trimmer

Manual grass shears

Sheep shears

Figure 3.3. Cutting Tools.

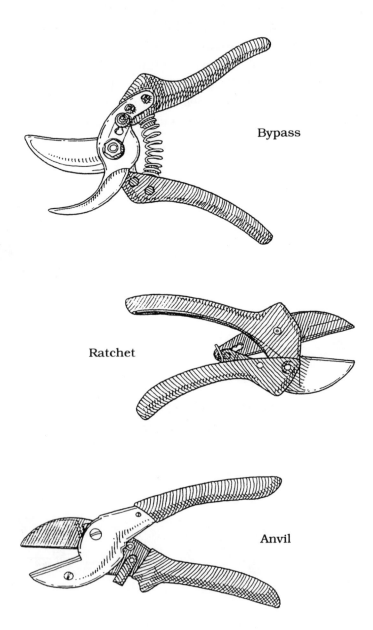

Bypass

Ratchet

Anvil

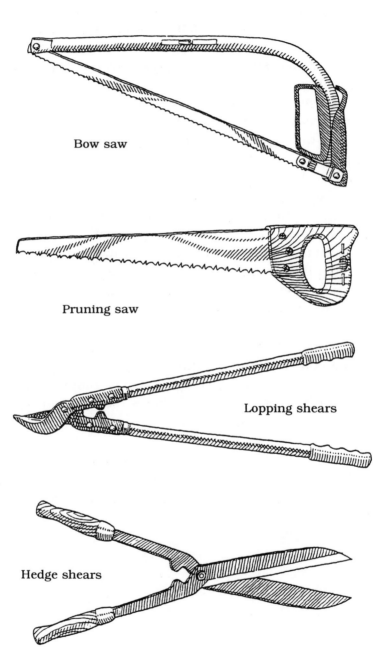

Bow saw

Pruning saw

Lopping shears

Hedge shears

into the base of the tool; a ratchet style, which works like the anvil but adds a mechanism that allows you to cut a large stem with successive cuts; and a bypass style, which seems to be preferred by professionals for clean cuts and durability.

Lopping shears are a must to have around the garden. Otherwise, you'll be tempted to use your hand-held pruner for big stems—and end up breaking the pruner. Lopping shears are useful for cutting woody stems that are a half-inch or larger in diameter.

Anything thicker than an inch and a half calls for a saw—either a pruning saw or a bow saw. A *pruning saw* is fine for smaller jobs (pick a blade with medium-sized teeth), but a *bow saw* will give you more support when making thicker cuts. This support is especially important for cutting evergreens, which have sappy wood that can impede the cutting motion and cause pruning saws to bend.

Finally, *hedge shears* will make your job a lot easier when you are cutting multiple stems of pliable plants, as when you're trimming hedges or removing the top layer of a bushy plant. Figure 3.3 shows the different types of cutting tools available.

Using the proper tool for each job will ensure that you get the job done efficiently. A few sturdy tools, made for durability, are a good investment for gardeners.

4

Back to Earth, the Living Soil

*The star player
of the biodynamic movement*

The environment of living plants is very complex and almost defies any complete study. Yet, there are certain physical forces that have a direct, easily recognizable effect upon the growth and development of plants. Soil, above all, plays the biggest role in biological management.

Soil biology is one of the most important, but least studied, aspects of soil science. You can tell what kind of soil you have by the vegetation that grows around the area. You know, for example, that there is acid soil by the presence of conifers, oaks, wintergreen, blueberries, mosses, rush, sorrel, and spurry. As a rule, soils in the Northeast tend to be less acidic than those of the Southeast. Soils in the Northeast developed under deciduous forests, which made them less acidic than soils that developed under the mixed conifer and hardwood forests more prevalent in the South.

SOIL LAYERS

To better understand your soil, take a look at its profile—a vertical slice of ground showing the various layers. With a handheld soil **auger** (a tool used for boring holes), you can twist through the soil just as you twist a corkscrew into the cork on a bottle of wine. Go down about 2 feet, and then carefully pull out the auger.

The top layer consists of decomposed and semi-decomposed organic matter and, in healthy soil, it is dark brown to black. Underneath is the **topsoil**, the layer of soil which is richest in organic material and in which plants generally have their roots. Topsoil varies in depth from a few inches to a few feet, depending on geographic location. Good topsoil is deep brown in color.

The next level down is the subsoil. In well-drained soil, this layer will have an orange color, indicating the effect of oxygen on the iron in the soil. This orange hue would show up in the topsoil, too, but the organic material hides the color. If your subsoil is grayish, the soil is lacking in oxygen, a sure sign of poor drainage.

KINDS OF SOIL

Soils are classified according to texture (the percentage of sand, silt, and clay), structure (the shape and arrangement of soil particles), and porosity (pore space).

Soil Texture

The texture of soil can be measured precisely through mechanical analysis. One method is to run a sample through sieves of varying screen sizes to separate large sand granules from small clay particles. But you can also get an indication of your soil's texture by rubbing it between your thumb and fingers. If it feels gritty, it is too sandy. Soil too full of silt, caused by glacial deposits, has a powdery feel when dry. Clay soils are harsh when dry and sticky when wet. The ideal soil is granular, with clusters that lie loosely in your hand and readily shake apart.

Soil Structure

Soil structure refers to granulation: Sandy soil, for example, shows little granulation. Excessive trampling by people or livestock, as well as the operation of heavy equipment, will affect soil structure by compacting the soil. Plants growing in compacted soil cannot develop heavy root systems; the soil must be loosened before planting can begin. On the other hand, too much tilling can break down the structure of many soils.

Porosity

Pore space is associated with both texture and structure. It refers to the air or water pockets sometimes caused by the removal of stones or minerals. Pore space is important because it aids drainage and allows needed oxygen into the soil. The reason you should never add sand to a clay soil is that the sand particles do such a great job of filling the thin ribbons of pore space found in clay; the result is cement.

SOIL TEMPERATURE

Another test of soil is temperature. Plants grow quicker in warm soil, which is why commercial nurseries will warm the bottom of their soil mix with coiled tubes filled with hot water.

Soil scientists have found that an organic mulch (see Chapter 8) decreases the fluctuations in temperature. It makes the soil warmer in winter and cooler in summer. The mulch also retains more snow, which further protects the soil against temperature extremes. Clay is a cool soil in summer because of the constant evaporation of moisture from its surface, which seldom gets dry.

HOW SOIL IS FORMED

To understand soil management, we must first understand our soil inheritance. Part of the process of soil formation involves the decaying remains of the low forms of plants, such as lichens and mosses, which covered exposed rocks by digging their tiny tentacles into the surface. This process slowly formed a film of soil over the rocks and provided a foothold for the plants of the next step on the evolutionary ladder—the ferns. Gradually, as the soil thickened, other plants began to grow.

Without soil organisms such as bacteria, fungi, and yeast, no soil formation could have taken place. The process continues to this day. Likewise, ants, termites, and beetle larvae serve as soil makers by speeding the decomposition of forest debris. Physical forces—heat, cold, rain, ice, wind, erosion, waves, and currents—also play a part in soil formation, as do the chemical excretions and respirations of microbes.

Specialists in organic farming have known for some time that the normal and natural condition of the soil should be disturbed as little as possible. The topsoil must be disturbed, of course, before planting, if only to turn under weeds and remove rocks. In addition, if there is a lot of clay in the soil, the soil needs to be aerated to make it porous. The best aerator of all is the earthworm, and you are ahead of the game if you have plenty of these creatures.

Topsoil can be 1 to 2 feet deep in the Corn Belt and 3 to 4 feet deep in the Great Plains, but it is much shallower in other parts of the country. In the Northeast, topsoil is usually no more than 6 inches deep. This layer contains minerals, organic matter, water, and oxygen. If you dig deeper, you find fewer and fewer of these nutrients. That's why it should be a rule of thumb never to plow so deep that the nutrient-poor subsoil is brought to the surface. Those who plow deep naturally must add more fertilizer.

THE WEED FACTOR

The condition of your soil is reflected in the type of weeds it holds. Nature has a reason for allowing weeds in the soil. The geographic region, the presence of clay, and the presence of limestone deposits all contribute to the weed factor. Organically rich soils encourage rapid growth, so plants can crowd out weeds. Clay soils, on the other hand, inhibit growth and make it hard for plants just to keep pace with weeds.

An overabundance of weeds shows a lack of soil fertility. Nature is simply trying to put some nutrients back into a starved soil. Fertile, well-conditioned soil has lots of organic matter and is not naturally conducive to weed growth. Some weeds thrive only in soil that is low in minerals or has an excess of other trace elements. Weeds seem to lose root systems in a soil rich in bacteria and organic matter.

The deeper you plow, the more weeds you will have, for their seeds exist deep in the earth and would otherwise stay dormant. But weeds tell us a lot about the soil. For instance, acid soils usually play host to sheep sorrel, swamp horsetail, hawkweed, corn spurry, and knapweed. Daisy, field sorrel, and doorstop weed inhabit slightly acid soil, whereas wild aster, wild lettuce, partridge pea, broom brush, yellow toadflax, and wild onions find a home in sandy soils. Limestone soils will give rise to pennycress, peppergrass, field madder, mountain bluet, and yellow chamomile. Poorly drained soils will produce smartweed, silverweed, meadow pink, hedge nettle, stinking willie, joe-pye weed, and many of the sedges.

Weeds are good in many ways. They bring up moisture and minerals from the subsoil, break up the hardpan, and let crops feed on anything in the lower depths that is good for them. They conserve nutrients that would otherwise be washed out or blown away from bare ground. They also aerate the soil and allow space for the roots of plants to spread.

SOIL ACIDITY

Soil is what you make it. However, it is good to evaluate your soil before you make plans to raise certain crops that require specific nutrients. For example, most plants do better when the soil pH is neutral. The **pH** scale is a numerical measure of acidity. A pH of 7 indicates neutrality; lower numbers mean increasing acidity, and higher numbers show increasing alkalinity (that is, decreasing acidity).

Very acid soil causes plants to become sickly and die. Yellowing is one sign of danger. It is safe to assume that most vegetables prefer lime, which is alkaline, and dislike acidity. Lime is also a great help to clay soils. On the other hand, in a sandy soil, lime has the effect of holding particles of the soil too close together, so that water is held for a longer time. Besides lime, other sources of calcium are bonemeal, **dolomite** (calcium magnesium carbonate), wood ashes, and oyster shells.

(For more specific information on adding nutrients to soil, see Chapters 7 and 8.)

BUILDING UP SOIL WITH GREEN MANURE

The oldest method known for building up soil is the rotation of crops. But soils can also benefit from **green manure**—crops that are planted specifically to be plowed under to benefit the soil. Although it is not a magic cure-all, green manure does take its place alongside organic matter and waste materials as a soil builder. If a soil contains mineral deficiencies or imbalances, green manure will correct them. Only one rule must be observed: The crop must not mature before you turn it into the soil. Why? Because as the green manure matures, its nitrogen content diminishes. In addition, the plants can also become troublesome weeds if allowed to go to seed.

Benefits of Green Manure

Green manure crops are usually low-priced seed and much cheaper than the average chemical fertilizer. Like mulch, green manure acts as an insulating blanket, keeping the soil warmer in the winter and cooler in the summer. This encourages soil life activity in general and earthworm growth in particular. The more earthworms, the more channels they will burrow deep in the subsoil, bringing to the surface useful minerals and nutrients that will increase the health and insect resistance of food crops. The roots of many green manure crops themselves reach deeply into the subsoil, where they absorb and bring up valuable minerals to revitalize the soil when the plants are plowed under to decompose. Green manure crops decay in the soil fairly quickly. In warm, moist conditions, decomposition is nearly complete in 6 weeks.

Using Green Manure

Let's assume the worst conditions. Say the land you want to improve consists only of subsoil or contractor's fill—in other words, you have a weedy lot. Follow this plan.

1. Plow under all the weeds, and allow the rough furrows to stand for 10 to 15 days.

2. Coarsely rake the area, or use a disking implement (a tool with several sharp blades attached to a handle, such as the tiller shown in Figure 4.1, available from a farm store) to slice repeatedly through the soil.

3. Sow a very thick crop of buckwheat. Even on the poorest land, the buckwheat will make a fair stand.

4. Let the buckwheat grow only about 8 inches; then turn it under.

5. Wait another 10 days; then sow another crop of buckwheat, which will germinate considerably better than the first.

6. Plow this growth under as well, and let the plot lie fallow until October.

7. Put in a heavy seeding of winter rye.

8. Plow the rye under in the spring when it is about 9 inches tall.

Green manuring need not be this intensive unless your land is really in bad shape. Sometimes a crop or two

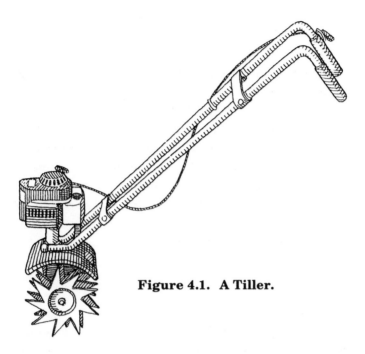

Figure 4.1. A Tiller.

will suffice to add all the **humus** (partially decomposed organic matter rich in nutrients) that the soil will need.

Nutrient Suppliers

While buckwheat and rye are good at improving the physical texture of soil, they add little real plant food. This is best accomplished by planting legumes such as pea, clover, vetch, and alfalfa. Plants used for green manures are of two classes: nitrogen gatherers (legumes), which put atmospheric nitrogen into the soil; and nitrogen consumers (nonlegumes), which use nitrogenous compounds already in the soil. The former are generally the most important because they increase the supply of this essential element of plant growth. Some **cover crops**—crops planted to improve the soil and not meant to be harvested—add as much as 150 pounds of nitrogen per acre of garden soil, or the equivalent of approximately 5 tons of manure. Nitrogen consumers, on the other hand, are favored for short-term production of organic matter.

Green manure supplies the soil with succulent organic matter at the peak of its nutritional benefit. Compost, no matter how carefully tended, will lose some of its nutrients to leaching and to the elements. (Compost is discussed in detail in Chapter 8.) But soil carefully treated with the green manure will hold nutrients, especially the minerals found only deep in the subsoil.

Crop Selection

The choice of your green manure crop will depend on the time of year. Some, such as cowpeas and buckwheat, require warm or hot weather for their development and are susceptible to frost. Others, such as rye and winter vetch, need cool weather and are resistant to frost damage. Rye can be planted any time after your last vegetables have been harvested. A good idea is to plant it between rows after the last cultivation. Kale, another green manure crop, can be sown in bare spots in late summer or early fall. Sweet clover, or melilot, has notable value as a green manure because of its deep rooting habit and its abundant foliage. However, if the soil is acid, the plant may fail unless lime superphosphate is applied shortly before seeding. Sweet clover gives best results if sown in late fall or on the snow during the winter. The plants get an earlier start than the weeds.

Rotating green manure crops from one season to the next will discourage plant disease and insects. (See Chapter

7 for more details on green manure.) Here are some good crops:

Legumes

- *Alfalfa.* Deep-rooted; does well in all but sandy, clayey, acidic, or poorly drained soils.

- *Clovers.* Many varieties for all soil types and climates.

- *Cowpeas.* Quick-growing; good soil builder.

- *Velvet beans.* Grown in the South; one of the best crops for sandy, poor soils.

- *Vetches.* Varieties for all climates; will grow in any reasonably fertile soil with ample moisture.

- *Soybeans.* Good for all soils, including acidic, and all climates.

Non-legumes

- *Barley.* Needs rich, loamy soil; grown mainly in the North.

- *Buckwheat.* One of the best for rebuilding poor or acidic soils; mostly grown in the Northeast.

- *Millet.* Does well in poor soils; mostly grown in arid regions of the South or Southwest.

- *Rye.* Grows well in all soils.

- *Wheat.* Needs fairly fertile soil; grown all over; several varieties.

- *Oats*. Needs mild winters; will grow in any soil with sufficient moisture.

Understanding your soil is the prerequisite to correcting any problems or deficiencies. The texture, structure, porosity, temperature, and acidity of the soil determine the gardening techniques you use and the crops you can plant successfully.

5

Companion Planting and Protective Botanicals

*How the buddy system
works in nature*

Companion planting is simply the placing together of growing plants that are beneficial to each other. It is a botanical buddy system that protects plants from insects and disease while making them healthier and more productive. This is an excellent way to bring the balance of nature into your garden and eliminate the need for deadly pesticides. Along with green manure, composting, mulching, and proper drainage, companion planting is one of the most important cultural practices in organic gardening.

For centuries, people have combined herbs with vegetables and some vegetables with other particular vegetables. Insect control is the most frequent reason given for such companion planting. Actually, the plants simply thrive better when they are with friends or companions. Plants grown among companions have increased vigor and less stress, so insects pass them by looking for weak or sick plants.

THE ROLE OF BACTERIA

The secret to companion planting lies in the soil, which J.I. Rodale, publisher of *Organic Gardening* magazine and a pioneer in organic farming, envisioned as a living, breathing organism. "Fire in the soil" was the way he described its teeming life. Nature has provided the nutrients in the soil; we have only to be good stewards to help plants use them.

Every garden has its growth stimulators as well as growth inhibitors. Plants interact with and influence each other. In the scheme of things, bacteria are ready to cause problems if nature's rules are broken. But bacteria also play other roles. They are instrumental in breaking down organic matter. They also prevent disease.

In addition, good **tilth** (cultivation) and a productive soil structure are the result of the activity of bacteria, which exude a gummy substance that binds the soil particles together. In a soil low in bacteria, the particles will not clump together as effectively. The proper clumping of soil is necessary for good cultivation.

PLANT COMPATIBILITY

Several factors determine which plants are compatible or incompatible. They include different requirements for moisture, aeration, nutrients, sunlight, and acidity. For example, some plants prefer full sun and some prefer shade. For this reason, pole beans can climb cornstalks, while tomatoes must be grown in the open. Different crops do better with greater or lesser amounts of nutrients and with higher or lower soil pH. Varying amounts of water in soil are required by different crops. Watercress likes to swim in water, but tomatoes are extremely sensitive to excess moisture.

Plant Rotation

A practice related to companion planting is crop rotation, which is done both for soil protection and disease control. Rotating crops helps prevent disease because the soil microorganisms that attack one crop will leave when a different crop is planted. These microorganisms are not allowed to build up to the destructive levels they would reach if the same crop were sown in the same area year after year.

Rotation also prevents a crop from depleting the soil with its specific demands of nutrients. All plants use nutrients, so it's good to include legumes in your rotation plan. Legumes store nitrogen in their roots; leave the roots in the soil and they will release nitrogen as they rot. Beans, peas, and clover are among the different types of legumes. (See Chapter 4 for more legumes and their properties.)

Plant Excretions

The plants that grow in soil not only absorb nutrients, they also exude substances. For instance, many gardeners know that planting walnut trees near rosebushes will kill the rosebushes. The walnut roots excrete a substance into the soil that is toxic to the roses and to some vegetables. Sycamore and wild cherry trees also inhibit vegetable growth.

Root Systems

Roots play another important role in companion planting. Plants with deep root systems enlarge the feeding area of shallow-rooted plants by plunging through compacted subsoil and loosening the ground. Consider the size of root systems when deciding which crops to plant together. It helps, too, if the roots of two plants occupy different strata, or levels, of the soil. Swiss chard and beans, or potatoes and beans, are compatible because they spread their roots at different levels.

CHOOSING PLANT COMPANIONS

A good rule when deciding which crops to put together is to pick plants that are opposites in some crucial way, such as their habits of growth or their shape. Celery and leek are compatible because the upright leek can find light near the bushy celery plant. Both are potassium lovers.

Another rule is to avoid grouping vegetables that have the same growth habits. For example, eggplants and peppers both grow above ground and therefore compete for the same nutrients. Instead of planting these together, you would pair plants that produce above ground with those that produce below ground, such as the garlic and spinach shown in Figure 5.1.

Plants with different growing seasons make good companions. You can put peppers in the same row as spinach, since one is harvested early and the other late. Lettuce and kohlrabi are good together because the lettuce will be harvested by the time the kohlrabi needs more space in the row.

In general, you can intercrop companion plants by growing them in the same row or by planting them in adjoining rows. Paths are best between sections rather than between companions.

**Figure 5.1. Spinach and Garlic Make Good Comapnion
Plants.**

Companion planting strengthens vegetables, giving
them better taste and less insect damage. Mix in a number
of aromatic and other herbs and you will have the benefit
of nature's true design of a healthy garden. Let's take a few
more examples. Peas like carrots, in part because one is a
topside vegetable and the other is a root vegetable. Always
leave the pea roots in the ground after the harvest to rot
and add nitrogen to the soil. Corn should have dill planted
on either side of each row. It will make the corn more
resistant to disease. Pumpkins and winter squash do well
between rows of corn. Tomatoes not only like basil planted
between them but also enjoy marigolds. Surrounding tomatoes with marigolds will keep away **nematodes** (microscopic worms that live in soil), which are great attackers of
tomatoes. Planting cabbage near tomatoes repels the cabbage fly.

Potatoes are one of the most fussy vegetables and they definitely do not like any of the vine family, including cucumbers and squash. Also, you will not want to plant sunflowers along a potato patch. Neither will do well. Beans should be planted between rows of potatoes. Horse-radish, too, benefits the potato patch and should be planted in the corners.

Radish seeds planted in the middle of the cucumber hills will make healthier cucumbers. Spinach likes straw-berries, turnips, and cucumber but not cabbage or any vegetable in the cabbage family. Beets like onions, but not tomatoes or pole beans. Celery likes beans and cabbage, and so on. Check the Companion Planting Chart on pages 52 to 53 for further help with companion planting.

HERBS AS COMPANION PLANTS

Herbs belong in every organic garden. It has only been since the Renaissance that flowers, herbs, and vegetables have been planted in separate gardens. Herbs are really the guardians of the garden because they protect the health of the plants and the soil. Their excretions, which are often antibiotic and fungicidal, are a protection against disease. And their natural use against an invasion of insects and plant diseases is well known.

American Indians taught early settlers much about the use of herbs in gardening. Basil and borage, for instance, should be planted near tomatoes. They not only protect against the tomato worm but also condition the soil with nutrients that tomatoes need. Marigolds should be planted profusely throughout the garden. They repel nematodes that infest many plants, especially root plants. Japanese beetles are repelled by rue. Tansy is good for so many things, from keeping ants out of the house to repelling cucumber beetles and squash bugs in the garden. Planting sage near carrots and cabbage will protect these vegetables from the carrot fly, the cabbage moth, and the cabbage fly. Thyme is also good protection against cabbage worms.

Nasturtiums are good companions to radishes and cabbages. Planted under fruit trees, they deter aphids and squash bugs. They also improve the health and flavor of vegetables. Yarrow is great along garden borders since it enhances the essential oils in plants. Rosemary likes cabbage, beans, and carrots and deters cabbage moths, bean beetles, and carrot flies. Tarragon is best planted throughout the garden. A border of wormwood will keep animals out. Savory, especially the annual summer savory, improves the flavor of beans and helps deter the bean beetle. It is not the most effective pest chaser, nor is it easy to grow, but savory is worth planting because it is a good cooking herb and makes an excellent companion for onions.

Asparagus does well with basil planted along its rows. Sage, the perennial herb commonly used for poultry seasoning, is another excellent repellent of insects in the garden, and it protects vegetables, particularly vine crops and members of the cabbage family. Sage is also good to grow with carrots.

Hyssop planted near grapes increases their yield. Valerian grown as a border helps most vegetables, since it stimulates the phosphorus activity in the vicinity. Spraying valerian tea on vegetables once a month encourages growth and helps fight insects and diseases. Make the tea by steeping dry leaves in boiling water until the water turns color. The herb is also attractive to earthworms and, therefore, helpful to the compost pile.

A few borage plants in the strawberry patch will help the fruit. It does spread widely, however, and must be kept in check. Borage is also an excellent border crop, providing potassium, calcium, and other minerals. Honeybees like to

Companion Planting Chart

	ASPARAGUS	BASIL	BEANS	BEETS	BROCCOLI	CABBAGE	CHAMOMILE	CARROTS	CAULIFLOWER	CELERY	CHIVES	CORN	CUCUMBER	DILL	EGGPLANT	FENNEL
ASPARAGUS		G														
BEANS					G			G	G	G	B	G	G			B
BEETS			G													
BROCCOLI			G							G				G		
CABBAGE			B	G						G				G		
CARROTS		G												G		
CAULIFLOWER										G						
CELERY			G				G				G					
CORN			G										G			
CUCUMBER		B					B								B	
EGGPLANT			G													
KOHLRABI			B	G												
LEEKS								G		G						
LETTUCE								G								
MUSKMELONS												G				
ONIONS			B	G	G	G										
PEAS			G							G		G	G			
PEPPERS		G														
POTATOES			G										B		G	
PUMPKINS												G				
RADISHES					G			G					G			
SQUASH												G				
TOMATOES	G											B				B
WATERMELONS												G				

	GARLIC	HORSERADISH	KOHLRABI	LEEKS	LETTUCE	MINT	MUSKMELONS	ONIONS	OREGANO	PARSLEY	PARSNIPS	PEAS	PIGWEED	POTATOES	PUMPKINS	RADISHES	SAGE	SQUASH	SUNFLOWER	TOMATOES
1										G										G
2		B			B				B						G				B	
3				G					G											
4									G											
5									G											B
6						G	G		G	G							G			G
7									G											G
8					G															G
9								G						G		G			G	
10			B				B									G				
11														G			B			
12						G			G											B
13									G											
14				G					G							G				
15																G				
16	G					G							B							G
17	B								B							G				
18			G													B			B	B
19						G		G				G						G		
20																	G			
21				B										G	B					

G = Good   B = Bad

feast on the blossoms. Flowering herbs are considered helpful because they attract bees to pollinate tomatoes, peppers, cucumbers, squash, beans, peas, melons, and berries. A border of lavender, borage, bee balm, or thyme will assure a steady hum of bees.

Most of the companion herbs have a strong aroma and exude equally strong flavors into the soil, making them good insecticides. Garlic, one of the most pungent, is a real bouncer of insects. You can sow it safely throughout the garden. Ring rose bushes with cloves of garlic and you'll see aphids disappear and the flowers brighten in color. Members of the aromatic mint family, particularly pennyroyal, operate on the same principle. Mints are especially effective against moths, ants, and fleas.

Chamomile, an herb considered medicinal for people, is also a physician in the garden. Herbalists have sung its praises for many years as a plant healer. A small chamomile root planted alongside sickly plants, including house plants, will improve their health in 10 days.

On the other hand, some herbs are poisonous to other plants. Beware of fennel. It is definitely a garden outcast and should not be planted near vegetables or other herbs. Dill doesn't like its cousin, the carrot. Hyssop and radishes are not on speaking terms, and there is no love lost between cucumbers and sage. Rue should never be planted near basil; they are antagonists. Perhaps this disharmony exists because basil is one of the sweetest herbs and rue one of the most bitter.

In short, companion planting helps plants grow and helps control both insects and plant diseases. Although it may seem like a science, companion gardening is simple once you make a garden plan that pairs plants together for their own benefit.

6

Insects:
Good and Bad

*Your best friend
or your worst enemy*

The aim of every gardener is to grow healthy crops that are insect- and disease-free, with a 100 percent return on the seed planted. Of course, nature provides no such guarantees. But biodynamic techniques give gardeners effective ways to control pests and increase crop yields. Natural pest control can be reasonably managed and is worth the effort involved. It is, after all, the difference between having healthy soil and chemical-free crops or facing the inevitable breakdown of the soil nutrients and the danger of ingesting pesticides.

UNDERSTANDING PEST CONTROL

There are three methods of natural pest control, the first being physical control—picking off and destroying insects and insect eggs that are on or near your plants. The second is mechanical control, such as putting screening over plants or using insect traps. The last is to use cultural and biological practices that make the garden unattractive to insects. This is the most effective of the three, but it must be established long before the arrival of pests.

One of the most important considerations is to make sure the soil is fertile. Nutrient deficiencies or imbalances encourage many plant pests. If a plant is unable to extract valuable trace elements from the soil, it becomes weak and susceptible to disease and pests. When plants are attacked by insects, nature is warning us about improper nourishment. By concentrating on improving the soil, organic farmers can produce vigorous plants that are more insect-resistant. Crop rotation, companion planting, and growing herbs in the garden are other effective pest-control strategies.

While good cultural practices are the way to win the war against destructive insects, there are many strategies for winning daily battles. Recognizing the "enemy" is the place to start. Chewing insects identify themselves by the patterns they eat into plants. Flea beetles make tiny holes, while weevils make angular openings. Sucking insects turn foliage yellow or leave it stippled with white or gray. Their eggs can often be seen on the underside of the leaf. You know you have red spiders in the garden if the plants have yellow leaves that are "cobwebby" or mealy on the underside. White streaks mean thrips, a pest that is common in plants from nurseries. Look out for aphids when leaves curl up or down. (Figure 6.1 illustrates several kinds of common insects.)

PEST-CONTROL CONCOCTIONS

Most pests can be controlled with homemade sprays or

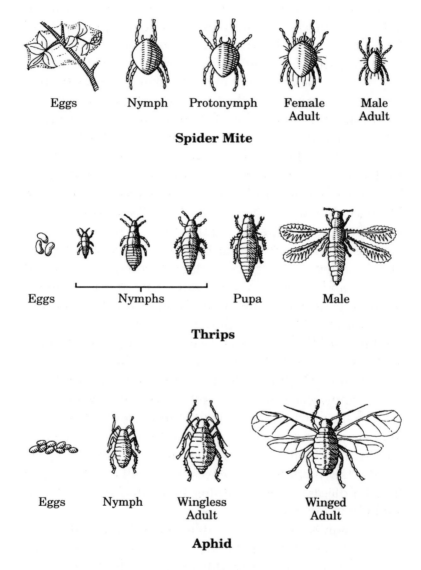

Figure 6.1. Some Common Insects at Various Stages of Development.

powders made from a number of ingredients, including garlic, horseradish, and wormwood. Store the mixtures in a dry, cool place. Use light amounts; hand sprayers work fine. Do not spray before or after rain. You want the plant to be dry. The best time of day to spray is at sundown.

Rhubarb leaves, toxic to man and bug, make a particularly good spray. Crush the leaves in 2 gallons of water and let the mixture stand for 36 hours. Strain and spray on plants infested with aphids, red spiders, or rose bugs.

Another all-purpose garden spray calls for one cup of fresh spearmint leaves and green onion tops, a half cup of horseradish root, and a few red peppers. Run them through a blender, and add water and just a drop of detergent. Detergent helps the spray adhere to the foliage.

Yet another spray can be made by combining in a blender a few garlic cloves, a tablespoon of mashed chili pepper, and a cup of warm water. Stir in a teaspoon of nondetergent soap. Spray this, strained, on any plant.

Spider mites, so tiny that it takes fifty to span an inch, can be controlled by a mixture of a half cup of buttermilk, 4 cups of wheat flour, and 5 gallons of water. This spray will kill not only the spider mites but their eggs as well.

Commercial sprays for apple scab are poisonous and destroy the nutrients in the fruit. A mixture of garlic, tansy, pennyroyal, and cloves is a better alternative. Crush the ingredients, blend in the oil, strain, and use as a spray. Raking fallen apples and leaves in the fall also helps control the disease. Good pruning helps too, since it lets in sunlight to kill fungi.

Cucumber beetles are deterred by a sprinkling of wood ashes around the base of a plant and on the lower leaves. Lime keeps away slugs and sow bugs. Slugs are attracted to acid soils, and their presence is a sure sign that your soil needs lime.

When all else fails, pick off the offending bugs, place

them in cooking oil and chop them in a blender. Spray the mixture on your plants.

OTHER PREVENTIVE MEASURES

In addition to using pest-control sprays and powders, you can employ other methods to prevent the growth of destructive pests. For example, to get rid of corn borers, cover some stakes with green paint and place them under the plants. Some people say the insects don't like the color green! Another trick is to use a variety of corn that matures in 80 days or delay planting until the last half of May. Burn any infected stalks.

Another common belief is that you should pinch off the bottom leaves of tomato plants before putting them in the ground. This is supposed to activate a plant hormone that is toxic to insects. Does it work? We're not sure. But we do know that chemical sprays destroy the nutrients in the soil, so why not take a chance on the folk tale and pinch off the leaves?

Removal and Cultivation

If insect damage to a plant is severe, the plant should be removed from the garden. But make one last effort before pulling it out: Plant a small chamomile plant next to the injured one, and in most cases, the plant will become healed. Chamomile is considered the physician of the garden and may be able to cure individual plants.

However, where there is a prevalence of sick plants, pull them out and cultivate the soil. Immediately work in either lime or bonemeal to kill the bacteria in the soil. Then skip a year before replanting the same crop in that area.

Insects that tend to attack certain vegetables often live and breed in the ground from season to season. They can be starved to some extent by the rotating of crops. Planting in the late fall—turning the soil thoroughly before the hard frost sets in—is fatal to many pests that would winter over in the soil.

Herbs

Like crop rotation and plowing, growing herbs in the garden is a proactive way to control insects. Pests simply do not like the scent or taste of many herbs. Garlic and marigolds, for example, deter a variety of bugs and should be planted throughout the garden. Planted around rose-bushes, garlic will deter aphids. Marigolds are especially effective against nematodes, microscopic parasites that infect the soil throughout the garden. Nematodes particularly enjoy root vegetables and can destroy whole rows of beets and carrots. Marigolds also discourage Mexican bean beetles and green tomato worms.

Mints are great for protecting the vegetables of the cabbage family. Winter savory not only protects beans from pests but improves their growth and taste. It is called the bean herb because it adds zest to the flavor of cooked beans.

The Artemisia family of herbs serves double duty as an aromatic ornamental and as an insect repellent. Living plants deter pests, but dried leaves or branches scattered around the garden produce the same effect. Varieties include silver mound, dusty miller, silver king, fringed wormwood, and the highly aromatic southernwood. Fennel and rue, on the other hand, should never be in the immediate area of garden vegetables.

A wall of yarrow planted around a garden will keep insects out. Catnip repels the flea beetle, and plant lice are deterred by pennyroyal. Hyssop planted near grape vines not only guards against insects but increases the yield of the grapes. Tansy planted under fruit trees will protect against both blight and insects. It is also a great companion to roses and raspberries.

Here's a quick guide to insect-repelling herbs:

- *Basil*. Repels any bothersome insect. Grow basil inside as a fly repellent.

- *Marigold*. Plant throughout the garden to deter nematodes, asparagus beetles, and most garden pests.

- *Pennyroyal*. Repels ants and plant lice. Rubbed on the skin, it is a protection against mosquitoes.

- *Rosemary*. Repels the carrot worm, butterfly, cabbage moth, and aphids.

- *Sage*. Protects against the cabbage fly, carrot fly, and ticks.

- *Savory*. Plant as a border around onions or beans to repel the bean beetle.

- *Tansy*. Repels fleas, ants, moths, beetles, and squash bugs. Rub into a dog's fur to repel fleas in the summer.

- *Wormwood*. Keeps away all predator animals. It also will repel cabbage insects. Spray a tea made of wormwood on the ground to get rid of slugs.

Companion Planting

Companion planting is another way to discourage pests. Planting radish seeds in the hill along with cucumber seeds, for example, will repel more insects. If the cucumbers are still having trouble, they may be under attack from a small beetle marked by three black stripes on its back. These beetles not only feed on the leaves but spread a bacterial wilt, bore into the roots, and feed on the stems. Luckily, marigolds will repel them.

Planting beans between rows of potatoes usually wards off the potato beetle as well as the Mexican bean beetle. Should this fail—the seed potato may have been grown in soil infested with larvae—scatter wheat bran on the plants in early morning before the dew disappears. The bugs will eat the bran and swell up like ticks until they fall dead.

Cinch bugs, which can destroy a whole patch of sweet corn, can be cleared out by the planting of soybeans as a ground cover. The same works for cutworms, the most common of all plant attackers and among the most destructive. They can chew and destroy more of a plant than they can eat. Crops planted on newly plowed sod land are especially susceptible to cutworms unless the land is plowed during late summer or early fall and is free of weeds.

Helpful Wildlife and Insects

Toads are a blessing because they consume cutworms the way baseball fans eat hot dogs. Some people mistakenly think that snakes are good for the garden. They are not. Snakes eat toads and frogs, which are more valuable in a garden because they eat more insects.

Before you declare biological warfare on your garden's pests, remember that there are also many good insects to be found there. Honeybees, for example, are important for pollinating plants. Some gardeners construct bee hives both to get a nice supply of honey—from 30 to 100 pounds per hive—and to increase their garden harvest.

Asparagus, artichokes, broccoli, cantaloupes, lima beans, and vine crops will benefit greatly from an influx of bees. Fruit trees are more likely to deliver a bumper crop if there are additional bees to help pollination in the spring. That's why many fruit growers request the service of bee-keepers.

Other good insects fall under two categories: predators and parasites. Predators prey on bad bugs while parasites deposit their eggs on bad bugs and allow the newborns to kill the host. Although it looks harmless enough, our friend the ladybug is a predator with a taste for aphids. The same with the lacewing, which feasts not only on aphids but on white flies, thrips, and mites. Parasitic wasps and even some flies—the hover fly and the tachinid fly may remind you of bees—will lay eggs on garden pests and start them down the road to ruin.

You can buy good insects, or you can attract them to the garden with the right mix of plants. Herbs and other plants with small flowers act as a beacon for good insects, providing them with an attractive home base. You can get a good start with a mixture of perennial daisies and other wildflowers, yarrow, Queen Anne's lace, dill, and fennel. Some gardeners will actually let a few of their broccoli and cauliflower plants go to seed, thereby providing yet another attraction to the good insects in the area.

Good gardening involves recognizing which insects are pests and which are friends. By using biodynamic techniques, you can deal effectively with pests without compromising your garden environment.

7

Fertilizers:
Understanding
Their Use

Finding the right balance
to benefit plants and soil

The objective of organic and natural fertilizers is to feed the soil, not the plant. Synthetic fertilizers do just the opposite: They feed the plant and starve the soil. Artificial fertilizers introduce some poisonous elements and create an imbalance with which it is hard for nature's forces to cope.

Plants grown on soils that have only minerals and no organic matter are like people forced to eat salty foods. They are driven to drink water and more water. Plants absorbing an excess of mineral salts also take in an excess of moisture. Though they look lush to the eye, they are no longer in balance and therefore no longer resistant to disease. Ultimately, crops will fail and the soil will be damaged and so drained of nutrients that no amount of synthetic fertilizer will help.

HOW FERTILIZERS WORK

Synthetic and organic fertilizers come from different sources. By strict chemical definition, "organic" means any substance containing carbon. But in the case of fertilizer, "organic" means the product is derived from plant or animal material, such as manure, bonemeal, and seaweed. "Natural" fertilizers contain inorganic materials that come from a natural source, such as rock phosphate, which is mined and crushed but not chemically altered.

Synthetic fertilizers are manufactured chemically. They provide the same nutrients as organic and natural fertilizers but deliver them in a more concentrated form. Nutrients in organic fertilizers are tied up in large molecules that must be broken down by soil bacteria before plants can absorb them through their roots. Synthetic fertilizers provide nutrients in simpler particles that plants can use right away, like a shot in the arm.

COMPOSITION OF FERTILIZER

Products sold in garden centers usually are identified as either "organic" or "synthetic." In addition, the label on each bag shows three numbers that indicate the relative proportions of nitrogen, phosphorus, and potassium. Add these numbers. If the total is higher than 15, it's likely that some of the ingredients in the product are not natural.

Whether organic or synthetic, a complete fertilizer should contain three essential elements: nitrogen, phosphorus, and potassium. Nitrogen helps promote leaf growth. Foliage plants such as spinach and lettuce generally require more nitrogen than flowering plants such as squash and eggplant. Organic nitrogen sources need warmth to be converted into a usable form. However, while nitrogen works faster in warm soil, it will last longer in cold soil. All nitrogen fertilizers will gradually acidify soils.

Phosphorus, sold in the form of rock **phosphate** or bonemeal, is important in the formation of seeds, fruits, and roots. It also makes plants disease-resistant. Potassium, often called potash, increases the strength of plant tissue, boosts winter hardiness, and promotes disease resistance. The most common source is muriate of **potash**, chemically known as potassium chloride.

HAZARDS OF SYNTHETIC FERTILIZERS

Synthetic fertilizers are generally cheaper than organic and natural products—they provide more bang for the buck. However, these high-test fertilizers are not good for plants in the long run. Crops do much better absorbing nutrients a little at a time, especially nitrogen. An overdose of nitrogen will spur foliage growth at the expense of the rest of the plant, weakening the roots and causing other damage.

The rush of nutrients from synthetic fertilizers also destroys pectin in both fruits and vegetables. Pectin exists to greater or lesser degree in all vegetables, not just apples or underripe fruit. In addition, synthetic fertilizers are water-soluble and more easily leached from the soil. A good rainstorm can leave plants starved for nutrients and can wash nutrients into ground or surface water, where they can cause long-term pollution.

Organic fertilizers, on the other hand, do not dramatically alter the chemistry of soil. They contain fewer salts than synthetic fertilizers and can be applied in larger amounts without damaging plants. They also promote the buildup of organic matter.

YOUR SOIL'S NEEDS

There are many natural sources of nutrients, including store-bought fertilizer, "waste" materials, and green manure. One organic fertilizer is no better than another, but some can give your plants more of the particular nutrient they need.

To find out which nutrients your garden needs, you can send in a soil sample for testing. A soil analysis will tell you what type of soil you have, what plants will grow best on it, and how to fertilize it. The analysis will also tell you the soil pH, which is important because the pH governs the availability of certain nutrients. An alkaline soil, for instance, inhibits plants from getting iron from the soil. Ask your local cooperative extension agent where nutrient analysis is done.

You can also look for clues in the weeds that sprout in the garden. Certain weeds signal nutrient deficiencies. (See Chapter 9 for a fuller discussion of weeds.) Crops also give signals when they need nutrients. Leaves on a corn plant will turn reddish purple if the crop needs more phosphate; the tips and middle vein of the leaves yellow when the corn needs more nitrogen. Annual soil testing is nevertheless a good idea, however, because it keeps you from applying too much fertilizer.

TYPES OF FERTILIZERS

The type of fertilizer you use depends on the nutrient balance of your soil and the requirements of your crops. But time and availability of materials are other important factors. Buying bags of organic fertilizer is the most practical option for some gardeners. These commercial products are made from a variety of materials, including bonemeal, blood meal, manure, paper mill pulp, and treated sewage. (Blood meal is blood, collected from slaughterhouses, that has been dried and ground.) Milorganite is sanitized sludge from Milwaukee's sewage treatment plant. Waste from the city's breweries gives it a unique composition.

Bonemeal

Bonemeal, a by-product from slaughterhouses, lasts longer in the soil than most other fertilizers and adds trace minerals and potassium. It contains at least 20 times more phosphorus than dried cow manure, yet bonemeal releases its nutrients very slowly while cow manure will release its phosphorus in one season.

Bonemeal, compost, or other organic materials should be added in the fall; some nutrients will penetrate the soil with the winter snow and rain.

Seaweed

Seaweed fertilizers have held high interest for years. Seaweed extracts not only promote more vigorous growth in crops, but also seem to protect plants from some insects. Seaweed and kelp extracts, both rich in trace elements, can be bought in undiluted liquid form or as granules.

Natural Minerals

Natural mineral fertilizers include rock phosphate and granite dust. Along with limestone, they are reliable sources of phosphorus and potassium. Hybro-Tite is one of the better-known rock products used by organic farmers. It comes from a gneiss rock mined in Georgia and has a mineral content of about 7 percent silica, 5 percent potash, 14 percent alumina (aluminum oxide), 1 percent lime, 4 percent soda, and 1 percent iron oxide. It also contains traces of many other elements. Hybro-Tite is not a substitute for either limestone or rock phosphate, but it works well with them.

Gypsum has been used as a soil conditioner and fertilizer for centuries. A calcium sulphate, gypsum is one of the key elements in many natural fertilization programs.

Humates, another fertilizer, have attracted notice among organic farmers. **Humates** are deposits of mineralized organic matter formed much the same way as coal. They contain high amounts of humus and generally are well-endowed with traces of minor elements. Navajos and Apaches used humates to grow corn in the southwestern desert at the time farmers in the Delaware tribe put fish in their hills of corn in the East. Settlers began using humates, too, but mostly abandoned them when commercial fertilizers became so convenient to use.

Other Sources

Other organic fertilizers are available closer to home. Ashes from the fireplace or wood stove make a good fertilizer, especially for root crops. Don't put them on potatoes, though. Wood ashes can encourage scab on potatoes.

Soot is another good fertilizer, but it should be made into a liquid form. Mix a quart to a barrel of water, and let the mixture stand a week before using it. Silt from brooks, streams, or ponds also is an excellent dressing for the soil, but it is exceedingly hard to handle in large quantities.

Burning crop residue left on the garden is another

form of fertilizing. It should not be done every year but is certainly recommended on alternative years, especially on a clay soil. Coffee grounds also are good for a clay soil, but they are best added to the compost bin. (See Chapter 8 for details about composting.)

Technically, any plant or animal matter that will break down in the soil and provide nutrition for plant growth is an organic fertilizer. However, most fresh material like food wastes, leaves, wood chips, and pulled weeds should be composted before being added to the garden. Compost is a wonderful source of organic matter for your soil but is too low in nutrients to be a good fertilizer. Organic matter is not thought of as a fertilizer unless its nutrients are in a concentrated form. Otherwise, it has too much bulk in relation to its nutrients.

Animal manure falls somewhere in between—it provides nutrients and adds organic matter to the soil. Just remember, fresh manure will burn plants, so it should be composted first. Manure from cattle, horses, sheep, and other cud-chewing animals contains more vegetable matter than that of poultry. Poultry manure has lots of power. We do not recommend using it, however, because poultry manure will explode under certain conditions. You must keep it cool by watering it down.

When we need to loosen our soil, as well as fertilize it, ruminant manure is the better choice. The only problem in using manure is not knowing whether it comes from animals that graze chemically treated fields or consume feed containing growth hormones and antibiotics. We believe this is often the case.

Because of concern over chemicals in animal manure, some organic farmers use only green manure. Green manure is a crop that is planted specifically to be plowed or dug back into the soil, enriching it with organic material and nutrients. This was a widely used practice in the nineteenth century, but it fell out of favor with the arrival of cheap chemical fertilizers. (For a discussion of how to use green manure, see Chapter 4.) Organic farmers who have rediscovered the technique are finding that the soil receives many benefits from manure that cannot be provided by other fertilizers.

Simply put, green manure is a way to provide organic matter for our gardens and fields from our gardens and fields. However, most green manure is only as good as the soil that produces it. If a soil contains mineral deficiencies or is low in organic matter, green manure alone will not correct the problem. That's because green manure is, for the most part, a closed system: The nutrients the plants take from the soil are put right back in. The exception is legume plants, which we will discuss in a moment.

Winter rye is the standard green manure crop to plant in the fall. Winter wheat or barley can also be used, but rye is preferred because it grows in cool weather, can be established later than wheat, and begins to grow earlier in the spring. Even if planted very late in the fall, rye will survive the winter as long as it germinates before the ground freezes. As soon as it's a foot high in the spring, it should be worked into the ground. Rye planted earlier in the fall can be worked into the ground before winter, and some gardeners plant it between rows after the last cultivation and weeding of late crops like cabbage and broccoli. Planting rye after late sweet corn is harvested is especially good since rye will replace the nitrogen corn takes from the soil. Midwestern farmers like to plant rye early in the fall so it will develop a good root system before winter. A cover crop of rye helps protect their open fields from winter wind erosion.

Kale is another good fall green manure crop. Sown in late summer or early fall, it will survive the winter and grow again the next spring. Legumes such as clover, alfalfa, and peas are good green manure crops because they have the ability to attract nitrogen-fixing bacteria to their roots. These crops draw nitrogen from the atmosphere and store it in their roots. When the plants are plowed under as green manure, this nitrogen stays in the soil to fertilize the next crop. Weeds can also be a green manure crop. The nutrient sponges of nature, weeds return plenty of good stuff to the soil.

Green manure is most effective when it is planted soon after the last crop is harvested and the soil cultivated. One authority, the Institute for Biological Husbandry in Switzerland, emphasizes that a green manure crop should be planted within 24 hours of harvest. Timing is also important when plowing under green manure. The crop should be worked into the soil when plants are still in a succulent stage of rapid growth. At that stage, the plants contain more nitrogen and decomposition is rapid; their nutrients are available to the next crop. If green manure crops are allowed to mature, their nitrogen content decreases and decomposition is slow. That's what the term "green manure" is all about: Plants must be green and succulent when they are worked into the soil.

Analyzing your soil and understanding its needs are the first steps in fertilizing. Using organic and natural fertilizers to add nutrients will ensure a healthy soil that produces strong, disease-resistant plants.

8

Composting
and Mulching

*Easy and efficient ways
to help your garden*

Compost and mulch are two of the best things you can give your garden. Although low in nutrients, compost worked into the garden is the premier natural fertilizer. This rich, organic material provides the most even distribution of nutrients and actually serves as a healing agent for the soil. Mulch laid down on top of the soil keeps in moisture, smothers weeds, and adds organic matter as it breaks down.

WHAT IS COMPOST?

Compost is any organic matter that has been allowed to decay into humus so that it can be used for fertilizing and enriching soil. When dug into a garden bed, compost increases aeration and helps the soil retain moisture and nutrients. Compost improves the root environment so much that it is better for plants than commercial organic fertilizers that contain more nutrients.

There's really nothing special about making compost. It's a natural process that has been taking place on the forest floor for as long as there have been forests. Human intervention simply speeds up the decomposition process. Yet composting is the ultimate in recycling. Organic waste from the lawn, garden, and kitchen is kept out of the landfill, converted into a useful form, and put back on the soil to produce more organic material. The transformation from life to death and back again takes place in the backyard compost pile.

MAKING COMPOST

Fortunately, composting is not a smelly affair. A properly managed compost bin or pile emits no odor other than the same earthy smell you get when you walk through the woods and kick up leaves. The heat generated by the decomposition process cooks out any bad smells and repels rodents. Even flies are rarely seen around a well-made compost bin. While raccoons may be attracted to compost piles, you can prevent their intrusion by covering the pile with a wire-mesh screen.

This heat, the "fire in the soil," is the essence of composting. Earthworms, bacteria, and fungi are the three builders of soil fertility and they require warmth to function effectively. The three create heat when they interact. Scientists call the process metabolism or oxidation, but this heat is a fire nonetheless.

The Compost Bin

Garden centers sell plastic compost bins and tumblers starting at around $100. These are good options for city gardeners with small lots and rodent problems. Otherwise, you can build one that works just as well and costs much less. Figuring out where to put the compost bin is the first step. Don't build it under a tree because that will be too damp. Compost needs as much exposure to sun and air as possible.

Some gardeners skip the bin altogether and simply make a compost pile on the ground. Others encircle their pile with snow fencing (wooden slats held in place with wire) or put it inside a square of cinder blocks stacked so air can circulate through the holes.

A compost bin shouldn't be more than 5 feet high, or it will be less productive and more difficult to use. We recommend building a compost bin of wood and chicken wire, such as the one shown in Figure 8.1.

1. Put down a single layer of concrete blocks.

2. Lay wood lattice over the blocks to form the bottom. The lattice should be heavy enough to provide support, but open to allow air circulation and drainage.

3. Lay a heavy wire netting over the lattice.

4. Create a wooden frame for the sides of the bin.

5. Staple chicken wire to the frame. Be sure the wire is taut, because if it starts to sag, the weight of the pile will pull the frame. (You can also use an old picket fence or snow fencing for the sides of the bin.)

6. Put a cover on the bin, even if it's just a sheet of plastic, so moisture can't get in and slow down the fermentation process.

Organic matter put into the bin or pile should be laid down in layers. Start with gravel or small stones, cover them with a layer of leaves or grass clippings, add kitchen scraps,

Figure 8.1. A Compost Bin.

and throw in a shovelful or two of soil. The soil is important because it contributes the worms, bacteria, and fungi
that will generate heat. Finally, sprinkle on a layer of lime
and you have the start of compost. Repeat these layers,
adding from time to time such things as sawdust, ashes,
garden residues, egg shells, and coffee grounds. Never add
animal products or any kind of fat—not even leftover salad
coated with dressing—because they will attract rodents.

A bin full of organic material must work, that is, mature,
for a year before it is ready to be used on the garden. You
should never have to turn, or mix, your compost if it is
properly layered. Layering will allow you to rest while your
compost cooks. But this method isn't always practical if you
want to compost all of your yard waste and kitchen scraps.

SUGGESTIONS FOR FILLING
YOUR COMPOST BIN

It's okay to toss things in at random, but try to keep a somewhat even mix of "green" and "brown" ingredients. Green ingredients are anything that was recently alive, like corn husks or stray plants pulled from the garden. Brown ingredients are items that have been dead awhile, like sawdust or the leaves you rake in the fall. Green things have more nitrogen, while brown things have more carbon. The microbes that will be feeding on your compost pile need a mixed diet of carbon and nitrogen. Some gardeners set aside bags of leaves in the autumn so they'll have enough brown to mix with all the green that will be thrown in the compost bin come summer.

Active composters will want two bins or piles, so one can cook while the other is being filled. But in this case, cooking means "stirring occasionally." Turning is necessary for an unlayered compost pile, both for aeration and to combine the green and brown ingredients. If you have a bin, use your pitchfork to give the ingredients a good stirring. If you have a pile, the best mixing method is to move the whole pile over a couple of feet, one pitchforkful at a time. It's not as bad as it sounds, especially if you keep your pile under 3 feet high.

The more you mix your ingredients, the quicker you'll get compost. A couple of good stirs a month will keep those microbes happy and healthy. But don't worry: The microbes will still work, although more slowly, even if you forget to turn your pile.

USING COMPOST

Sooner or later, you'll have compost. You'll know it's ready when the individual ingredients, such as leaves and apple cores, have disintegrated beyond recognition. The resulting humus should be crawling with earthworms—gold for the soil.

Compost is generally dug into the soil. Distribute the compost evenly on the ground. Then take a spading fork and dig it into the ground. Lift the soil and compost together, and then turn them over together.

WHAT IS MULCH?

A **mulch** is any substance, including plastic tarp, that covers the ground around plants and between rows. Some gardeners use compost for mulch. Mulching should be standard practice in all gardens.

Benefits to Soil

A thick mulch suffocates most weeds, making it a labor-saving device that many gardeners prefer to cultivation. In addition, a good mulch reduces by at least half the water lost through evaporation. It maintains uniform soil moisture, which helps root activity and nutrient movement. Potassium, which tends to stay near the surface of cultivated soils because the bare surface is alternately wet and dry, penetrates much deeper in a mulched soil that is more consistently moist. Over a period of years, hay and straw mulches will supply substantial amounts of potassium as they rot.

Organic mulches prevent low-hanging vegetables and strawberries from splashing in the soil during rainstorms. In the spring, when the ground is soft and muddy, a mulch makes it possible to walk close to plants. A mulch will keep heavy soils from becoming compacted when walked on soon after rain. Mulch also slows runoff and soil erosion caused by heavy rains. Rain soaks into an organic mulch more rapidly because the physical condition of the soil already has been improved. As it decays, mulch works down into the soil to make it friable and more easily penetrated by water. Rotting mulch also aerates the soil, thus stimulating root and biological activity. In addition, mulch helps prevent root injury because it eliminates the need for deep cultivation and hoeing.

Benefits to Plants

Mulch prevents disease in some crops, such as tomatoes. Tomatoes often get blossom-end rot under clean, cultivated soil. Mulched plants have few if any rotted fruits.

Research by Dr. Roy K. Simons, professor of pomology at the University of Illinois, has shown that mulching dwarf apple trees can double fruit yield. When you are planting dwarf root stocks, it is essential to keep the soil surface covered to protect the shallow roots from extreme temperatures. The mulch should be a thin layer of continually decomposing material that will improve soil conditions for the root system. By replenishing the mulch every two years, growers don't have to apply a lot of mulch at one time.

Some researchers are experimenting with mulches of different colors. Preliminary results suggest that the color of mulch could have a profound effect on plant size, yield, production, and perhaps even flavor. Plants read the light waves that are reflected off the mulch; different light waves tell plants to do different things. For example, research shows that green mulch makes tomato plants respond as if there were competing plants in the area. The crops grow taller and put out thin leaves that contain extra chlorophyll and use light more efficiently. A blue-colored mulch sends signals that stimulate plants to grow larger roots.

TYPES OF MULCHES

Using blue plastic is the only way to get a blue mulch. Commercial growers often use plastic mulch because it keeps the soil warmer in the spring and gives summer crops like tomatoes and peppers a head start. However, we generally recommend using organic mulches because they condition the soil.

Effective Mulches

Dry grass clippings make excellent mulch when spread in a 3- or 4-inch layer. Straw, salt hay, partially decomposed leaves, or compost also work well. A layer of newspapers, several sheets thick and weighted down with topsoil, also makes a good mulch.

Rapidly decaying mulches, such as legume hay and ground corn cobs, are much more effective than slowly decaying ones such as peat moss. Sawdust is an excellent choice, if it is available. Any sawdust is suitable, hardwood or softwood, as long as it has been seasoned. Wheat, rye, and oat straws are standard mulches for strawberries.

Leaves as Mulch

Tree leaves are probably the most common mulch because they are so plentiful. If you don't get enough from your own trees, you can beg some from your neighbors or collect the bags of leaves set out on curbs in the fall. A leaf mulch conserves moisture very well, and the only weed that pushes through is the ever-present birdweed. Of course, if you are lucky enough to pick up maple leaves, you will get thousands of seedlings that push their way to the top.

Remember that you must be careful when stockpiling leaves, straw, or other material to be used later as mulch. If the materials aren't stored properly, they can become acidic or sour. A sour mulch can damage plant tissue and alter soil pH.

How can you determine if organic mulch has soured? The quickest way is to smell it. Sour mulch usually has a penetrating odor much like vinegar, ammonia, or sulfur. In contrast, good mulch smells like freshly cut wood or garden soil. Another way is to check the soil pH. Sour mulch has a pH of 1.8 to 2.5, which is too acidic to be economically neutralized by lime.

Piles of mulching material should be allowed to breathe to prevent infestations of microorganisms. Keep piles small, because the larger the pile, the harder it is for fresh air to reach the center. Also, it's important to keep piles dry because mulching material will compress if allowed to become soggy. Compression prevents proper aeration.

USING MULCHES

Mulch should be applied early in the spring when the soil is moist. Ground mulched when dry is apt to stay dry if rain is sparse. Push back the mulch when you're ready to plant.

It is common practice to mulch flower beds over the winter to protect tender bulbs from frost. However, mulches should not be overly heavy, or they will compact the soil. The best time to mulch is in the fall. Limit the depth of the mulch to about 2 inches.

Compost and mulch are two of the most effective tools that gardeners have for improving soil and promoting healthy plant growth. Developing your own compost and mulch will enable you to really care for your garden's well-being.

---
(9)

Wild Plants: Protecting Their Usefulness

A look at worthy weeds

We do not view weeds as a detriment to the garden. Instead, they are potentially useful plants waiting to be discovered. Believe it or not, most weeds and wild plants are friendly herbs.

Native Americans knew this and did not grow crops without weeds alongside. They believed that the weeds that came up with a particular vegetable were good for that vegetable. Potatoes grown in weeds do better than potatoes in neat, clean patches. In China, weeds are considered treasures and women can be seen crawling over the hillside gathering such things as thistle, milkweed, and spurges to plant alongside their vegetables to feed the soil. Some weeds are ornamental. Although homeowners wage war against them, dandelions look spectacular massed in a field.

THE USEFULNESS OF WEEDS

Weeds both fertilize and condition the soil. Theories that they rob the soil of nutrients needed by crops are untrue. Common weeds have vigorous root systems that reach down into the subsoil for much of their mineral food. They bring these minerals up to the topsoil and make them available to crops, in effect collecting nutrients that would otherwise be washed away.

Weeds also draw moisture out of the subsoil. Water moves up along the outside of weed roots to the surface soil. These same deep root systems loosen the soil, making it easier for other crops to spread their roots. Corn and foxglove are good companions because the roots of the foxglove open up the soil so the corn roots can grow deeper.

Because they are rich in nutrients, weeds make good green manure. They are sensitive monitors of the health of your soil. Weeds can also heal plants because they generate heat. Place a sick houseplant in the middle of a patch of weeds and watch it thrive.

CONTROLLING WEEDS

Despite their many beneficial qualities, weeds should not be allowed to run rampant. Even on a patch of ground purposely allowed to grow wild—it will fill in quickly because nature abhors bare ground—the weeds must be thinned, and tall weeds, such as lamb's-quarters, should be topped. Weed patches should be rotated every two years to prevent less-valuable weeds from taking over. Otherwise, the deep-root weeds that condition the soil will give way to grass.

Grasses are troublesome weeds, and quack grass is one

of the worst. Also known as couch grass, wheatgrass, knotgrass, and witchgrass, it is most prevalent in the northern United States and Canada. Unlike many other weeds, such as crabgrass, foxtail, and barnyard grass that grow fresh from seed each year, quack grass is a long-lived perennial. It is one of the first plants to start growing in the spring and one of the last to die down in the fall. It sprouts in clumps with single-spiked seed heads and creeping rhizome roots that grow coarse and white, sending up a new plant at every node. Digging out the roots with a spading fork is the surest way to get rid of them. Tillers are no help because they only chop up and spread the roots. The best control is to prevent quack grass from ever getting a foothold.

A cover crop of buckwheat, properly planted, will vanquish most weeds, even quack grass. Another way to get rid of weeds is to cover them with mulch. Like all plants, weeds need sunshine to flourish. Cut off light and the most intrepid thatch of chickweed or creeping Jennie will get the message.

BENEFICIAL WEEDS

A number of weeds are welcome around the garden. Plants that make good soil conditioners include pigweed, lamb's-quarters, nightshade, ground-cherry, purslane, stinging nettle, and clover, the aristocrat of all weeds. All make good green manures if turned into the soil when they're young and succulent. Several types of weeds are illustrated in Figure 9.1.

Ragweed enlivens the soil. Saw thistle, which is really wild lettuce, makes a fine green manure in the fall. Sunflowers put down deep roots to draw nutrients from the subsoil. They also make good green manure because their

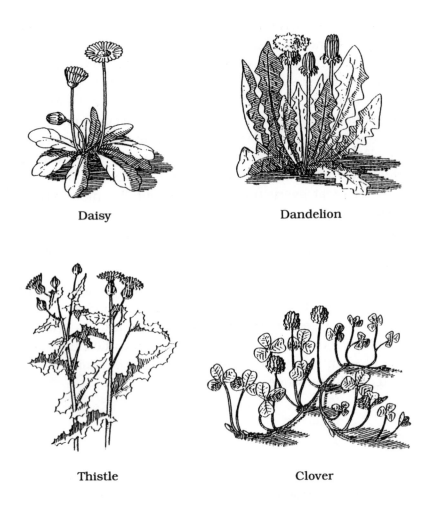

Daisy

Dandelion

Thistle

Clover

Figure 9.1. Some Common Weeds.

stalks disintegrate quickly. Milkweed should be encouraged because it is a vigorous growing perennial with a root system that wanders far from the base of the mother plant.

Dandelions, hated by so many, actually heal the soil by transporting minerals, especially calcium, from the subsoil. Their taproots can penetrate even a hardpan, a layer of compacted soil that thwarts the roots of most crops. However, dandelions give warning that there is a soil deficiency. Daisies, which are rich in calcium, signal that the soil lacks lime.

In addition to being a good soil conditioner, lamb's-quarters is one of the most nutritious of vegetables and tastes like spinach. It is actually a friendly weed; its leaf spread helps distribute water, and the deep root system brings minerals to shallow-rooted neighbors.

Most gardeners remove nettles, but these plants also have important benefits to the garden. Nettles secrete formic acid and add many minerals to the soil, protecting plants from disease. They help tomatoes, marjoram, and sage, among others.

Joe-pye weed, or boneset, grows in wetlands but has beautiful dusky-rose blossoms in the fall. Unlike many wildflowers, the blossoms of boneset stand up well in bouquets. Tall meadow rue has an airy blue-green foliage which resembles that of the maidenhair fern. It grows to 5 or 6 feet, requires a rich, moist soil, and self-sows in light woodland.

Mullein, also known as flannel plant, is another field weed with valuable properties. A classical herb, it was brought from Europe for its medicinal qualities. Mullein tea was traditionally used to treat colds and throat problems. The plant has thrived here, growing 3 to 8 feet high in vacant lots, in fields, and along highways from one end of the country to the other. In its first year, it puts down a large rosette of wooly foliage; it tops this the second season with a long, tapering spike covered with small, yellow flowers. The bottom leaves are larger than the top, and both stem and leaves are covered with tiny hairs that give them a velvety feel.

The beautiful perennial goldenrod is another herb thought to possess great healing powers. Herbalists have used it to treat everything from periodontal disease to flatulence. Unfortunately, goldenrod has been falsely accused of causing hay fever. The culprit is actually the pollen of the ragweed, which usually grows beside it.

Weeds are actually herbs and are experiencing a flurry of popularity as garden plants. Gardeners find these native species appealing because they will bloom year after year with very little work or worry. Many of them thrive on poor soil and, if they are carefully planted in an area similar to their natural habitat, can provide color and attract birds and beneficial insects.

10

Biodynamic
Lawn Care

Watching the grass grow,
naturally

Spreading chemicals on the lawn is almost as much of a tradition in the United States as eating turkey on Thanksgiving. Even people who use no chemicals on their herb and vegetable gardens find it difficult to break the habit of zapping their lawns with fertilizer and weed killer. But at what price? The perfect lawn to impress your neighbors may cause life-threatening complications for you, your pets, and your children.

Dr. Doris Rapp, professor at the University of Buffalo, has blamed lawn chemicals for breast cancer, learning disabilities, and asthma deaths. A study from the National Cancer Institute says that dogs whose owners hire lawn services to "sanitize" their lawns are twice as likely to get malignant lymphoma as dogs whose owners do not. Indeed,

we have a friend who believes she has lost two dogs to
"lawn care."

LAWN CARE SERVICES

Don't trust a lawn care service that says its chemicals are
safe. Ask what the chemicals are supposed to kill. A chemical that kills anything in your yard isn't safe. The federal
Environmental Protection Agency banned the use of the
insecticide Diazinon on golf courses and sod farms because
of widely reported bird kills—like the death of 800 wild
geese on a Long Island, New York, golf course in the 1980s.
But its use is still legal on home lawns!

Lawn service representatives may tell you the chemicals they use are registered with the EPA, but registered
chemicals are not safe chemicals. Registration means only
that the EPA has determined that the chemical will not
have unreasonable effects on the environment; the impact
on pets and humans is not mentioned. All eighteen of the
most commonly used lawn chemicals are now under new
evaluation for registration because of documented evi-
dence of detrimental effects.

Fire the lawn service expert who says he will "take
care of everything." He only wants to give your bushes
soup-bowl haircuts and saw off the long, graceful limbs
that swoop down with great expression from your favorite
trees. The advice and recommendations of lawn care "experts" often exceed their knowledge.

For example, many lawn care experts can't wait to
surround your shrubs and trees with wood chips. This
might control weeds, but fresh wood chips drain nutrients
from the soil as they slowly break down. They also provide
a great environment for breeding carpenter ants and termites. Of course, your lawn care expert hasn't warned you

about this. A lovely green ground cover would do just fine—and it would blend in with the natural surroundings. Composted leaves are also a better idea in most cases.

THE NATURAL LAWN

Why the fetish about the strip of green in front of your home? What's wrong with some dandelions, clover, or— horror of horrors—a bare patch? We say, dare to be natural. Make a silent agreement to preserve, protect, and encourage all the vagaries of nature.

Biodynamic lawn care is the answer. Like biodynamic gardening, it can be boiled down to three basics: Study the conditions in your yard, plant the most suitable grasses, and help them thrive with proper care. If your yard is healthy, crabgrass and dandelions will have a harder time putting down roots. Some weeds may find their way into your lawn despite your best efforts, but turf experts agree that good gardening practices should keep unwelcome plants under control.

PREPARE THE SOIL

Start the analysis of your yard with a look at your soil. Dig up shovelfuls at several spots around the yard, and check the texture of the soil. Is it sandy? Lumpy with clay? Or are you lucky enough to have dark brown, crumbly soil? Look for earthworms and organic matter in the soil. Soil around a new house may be rocky and barren, depending on how careful the builder was about replacing the topsoil displaced during construction. Trucks and bulldozers may also have compacted the soil. (See Chapter 4 for more details on soil treatment.)

As long as you're digging, take some soil samples and have them tested for pH. Acidic soil will need an application of lime. Some people sprinkle lime on their lawn every year out of habit, but biodynamic gardening demands more attention to conditions. It's better to either test your soil periodically or study the weeds in your yard for clues to your soil's pH.

If you're planting sod or seed on bare ground, loosen the ground first and work in organic material like compost or peat to improve soil texture. There's not much you can do to enhance the texture of the soil underneath established turf, other than deeply aerating the ground five to ten times.

PLANT THE RIGHT GRASSES

Consider the soil characteristics in choosing grasses. Sandy soil doesn't hold water, so grass will be less susceptible to diseases brought on by damp conditions. But because water leaches nutrients when it drains through sandy soil, the lawn may need extra fertilizer. Fescue varieties are good for loose, sandy soil because they have longer roots that secure the grass and pull moisture and nutrients from deep in the ground. They do well in shade and require less nitrogen than Kentucky bluegrass or creeping bent grass.

Sunlight

The ratio of sunshine to shade is one of the most important conditions in determining which grass varieties are best suited to your yard. In areas that get very little sun, you can try a fescue, but your best bet is to give up on grass altogether. In the long run, a bed of shade-loving perennials like ferns or hostas will be much less work. The same goes for a steeply sloped area or a drainage ditch. Save your back and your lawn mower, and plant pachysandra or other ground cover.

Traffic and Moisture

Other considerations are the amount of traffic you'll have on the lawn and the amount of moisture the lawn will receive, both from rain and the sprinkler. A good salesperson or a county extension agent can help you weigh these factors and choose the best type of sod or seed. He or she will probably recommend a blend of varieties as insurance against disease. Kentucky bluegrass is a hardy plant, well-suited for the pounding of an athletic field, but if that is the only type of grass you have, a bluegrass fungus could end up destroying the whole lawn. Mix in another variety and you'll cut your losses.

Seed and sod merchants may be cautious about suggesting the newest varieties, including strains of prairie grass, if they have not been tested in your area. However, you might want to experiment with these grasses, many of which require less mowing and watering than traditional varieties. Some of the newer varieties have improved disease resistance. The better cultivars are also naturally resistant to sod webworms, armyworms, billbugs, and cinch bugs because they contain a substance so bitter that it naturally repels blade suckers. When you are ordering, make sure to specify certified seed so that you get an improved variety and not a cheap blend.

Timing

Early spring or late summer are the best times to sow seed or lay sod. That gives the grass time to establish itself before the summer heat or the winter cold. New grass needs extra moisture and would do better to have five light waterings a day than one heavy downpour. Fertilizer high in phosphorus and potassium—the second and third numbers on the fertilizer bag—will help new grass bulk up its root system.

MAINTAIN THE LAWN PROPERLY

Planting the right kind of grass is half the battle; proper maintenance does the rest. Unfortunately, unlike the perennials you plant in shady or hard-to-mow parts of the yard, grass requires regular attention. Without human intervention, little grass would grow east of the Mississippi River. Abandon a lawn and it will revert to forest as quickly as the trees can grow. Even on the Great Plains, where grass is the natural vegetation, the prairie is healthier when it's burned off in an occasional fire or chewed down by a wandering herd.

No matter where you live, you're going to have to work with your lawn. That means giving it the correct amount of nutrients and water, and keeping it properly mowed and aerated.

Fertilizing

Fertilizer seems to be the trickiest part of this equation, and many people use much more of it than they need. Farmers like to say that they'd go broke in a week if they used as much fertilizer on their crops as suburbanites put on their lawns. And they're right. While farmers are becoming increasingly sophisticated about giving plants only as much food as they can use, homeowners continue to pour fertilizer on their lawns by the bagful. Not only does this damage their lawns, it could hurt the environment if excess fertilizer runs off into streams and lakes or leaches into groundwater. Because commercial growers were too liberal with fertilizer in the past, many wells in farming areas have been so contaminated by nitrogen that they can no longer be used.

For grass, use a fertilizer with more phosphorus and potassium than nitrogen. (For details on purchasing fertilizer, see Chapter 7.) Give your grass extra nitrogen by leaving clippings on the lawn. They break down quickly and do not cause thatch problems. Some people also add a top dressing of compost to their grass several times each growing season, taking care not to add more than a quarter-inch at a time.

Organic lawn care companies generally apply fertilizer two to five times a season, although some people claim a well-aerated lawn requires much less. Homeowners should experiment to see what works best for their lawns, but in general, more is not better when it comes to fertilizer.

Mowing

How you mow the lawn is important, too. Cutting the grass too short will prevent it from developing a strong root system. Raise the blades on your mower to keep your grass at least 3 inches tall. Cut the grass regularly, and keep the mower blades sharp so they slice, not rip, the grass stems.

Watering

Excessive watering can be harmful. Unless it's extremely hot, most lawns need only about a half-inch of water every 2 or 3 days. Use an empty tuna fish can to measure how much water your lawn gets from rain and the sprinkler. Morning is the best time to run the sprinkler because grass watered in the evening stays damp overnight and can be hit by a fungus. You may choose not to water at all during the hottest, driest part of the summer, when grass naturally goes dormant. In a normal year, a mature, healthy lawn will come back on its own when the rain returns.

Aerating

Aeration is one of the nicest things you can do for your lawn, and experts say you should go deep and often. Flattening it with a heavy roller is one of the worst things to do because it squeezes oxygen out of the soil and suffocates the helpful microorganisms that live there. Bowing to homeowners who like the striped effect of a rolled lawn, some lawn care professionals will run an empty barrel over grass, leaving stripes but not compacting the soil.

Aeration equipment—such as the tools shown in Figure 10.1—pulls out plugs of turf and dirt, allowing oxygen and nutrients to reach the microorganisms and work faster to break down thatch, the mat of dead stems that smothers new growth. Aeration reduces thatch much better than a power rake, which can hurt new grass. You can rent aeration equipment at a garden rental center.

Weeding

Doing all these things right still does not guarantee a

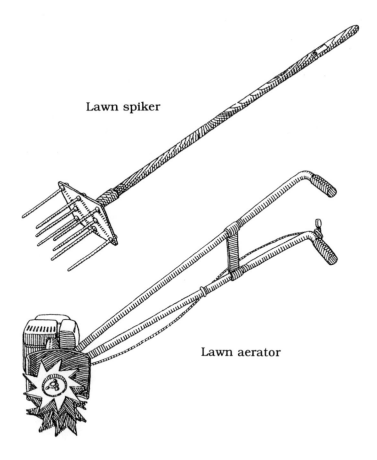

Lawn spiker

Lawn aerator

Figure 10.1. Aeration Equipment.

crabgrass-free lawn, especially the first year without the Weed'n'Feed. A particularly intransigent patch of weeds can be dug up and the area replanted with grass seed. Hand-weeding is more successful in the spring and fall, when grass can more quickly fill in the spot left by a yanked dandelion. Weeds, the ultimate survivors, thrive in the summer when grass is stressed by heat and drought.

However, they will have a difficult time ever taking over a lawn that is properly cared for.

By preparing the soil and planting the right variety of grass, you can have a healthy lawn without the labor and expense associated with a traditional grass lawn. More importantly, you will be contributing to a healthful environment for yourself, your family, and your community.

11

Managing Fields
and Woodlots

*The true worth of fallow fields
and forgotten forests*

Part of the biodynamic gardening plan
should include managed woods and fields.
Many of the same principles employed for
gardens and lawns can be used profitably for fields and
woodlots.

FENCE ROWS

The old argument that a clean fence row (one stripped bare
of vegetation) is necessary to control insect pests and
weeds doesn't hold true. A fence row of shrubs contains
more beneficial insects, birds, and small mammals than
one without bushes.

When incorporating shrubs and other woody plants
into a fence row, plan according to the habitat of quail

and other types of birds. Choose fence lines that will not be changed, and use plantings that will constantly harbor birds and other wildlife. Bayberry, chokeberry, high-bush blueberry, honeysuckle, autumn olive, and viburnum are excellent fence shrubs. Hardy and attractive shrubs typically found at nurseries, such as lilac and spirea, also are a good bet.

Before the advent of barbed wire, some farmers planted fence rows of Osage-orange trees, which are not only hardy and wind-tolerant but spiny enough to keep animals in check. Livestock like to eat the orange-like fruit. According to an old wives' tale, cockroaches will avoid a room containing an Osage-orange fruit.

Gullies, sinkholes, rock outcrops, and good land cut off from a field by a stream, gully, or drainage ditch are suitable locations for shrubs that provide food and shelter for birds and other wildlife. The same goes for field corners and borders.

An alternative to the deliberate planting of protective shrubs and food plants is leaving the strip uncultivated. Nature will take its course, and the strip will revert to natural vegetation in little time.

FIELDS AND MEADOWS

What is often referred to as a meadow is more likely an old field in a state of early succession. Left undisturbed, it is destined to become woodland in many regions. One exception is in the Great Plains, where trees don't grow without human intervention.

How Fields Evolve

When cropland has been abandoned, grasses and other

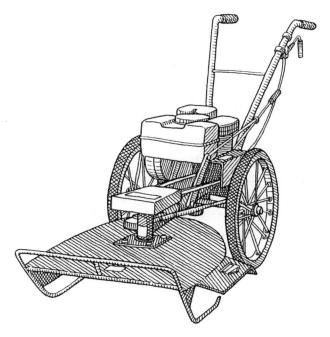

Figure 11.1. A Brush Mower.

herbaceous plants colonize the field and make it a
meadow. But these early colonizing plants are soon shaded
out by woody plants. Colorful wildflowers give way to
wild shrubs and then to short-lived poplar and sumac
trees. Later, rapidly growing silver maple and box elder
trees appear, followed by the climax forest of either conifer
or hard maple, beech, oak, and birch. If it's a meadow you
want, annual mowing with a brush mower (see Figure
11.1) will be necessary to keep woody plants from developing past the seedling stage.

The Virtues of a Meadow

There's increasing interest in growing low-maintenance

meadows instead of the ecological desert known as a lawn. The reasons are plentiful. For one, natural meadows attract wildlife, particularly butterflies and songbirds. In the springtime, ground-nesting birds rear their young in the cover of grassland. And summer flowers attract insects, which, in turn, attract birds. Autumn provides a bounty of highly nutritious seed for songbirds and their migratory cousins, while winter offers scavengers a chance to forage through the remaining storehouse.

Prairie vegetation is especially hardy. Most native meadow and prairie wildflowers are perennials that can grow on a variety of soils and put up with difficult conditions. It's not unheard of for some perennials to live 25 years. Drought does little harm to native meadow plants, which either continue to grow and flower or go dormant until it rains.

Meadow Plants

Wildflower seeds are commercially available in a variety of mixes. Packages containing mostly annual seed will give the restless gardener something to cheer about in short order, while perennial wildflowers are better suited for those in it for the long haul. A mix of annuals, biennials, and perennials is a good idea, and don't fret if the mix includes grass seed. Grass will fill in the space between flowers and provide a suitable backdrop for the floral show. Then, in the fall, grasses put on their own show of colors when they go to seed.

Short-growing grasses like sheep's fescue and hard fescue are preferable because they won't be too invasive. Grasses that form clumps, such as little bluestem, side oats grama, and Indian grass are a good match for natural flowers because they leave plenty of space for their showy neighbors.

WOODLOTS

Like a meadow, a woodlot also needs some human attention. Most people simply enjoy the woods without giving much thought to their well-being. Poets value the tranquility of woodlands, and hunters revel in the game. Others are satisfied to take a stroll through the woods, provided they don't come across any poison ivy. But if you're blessed with some woods of your own, there are ways to make a good thing better.

Inventorying Trees

The first thing you need to do is learn about the trees. Buy or borrow a book to help you identify what's out there. (See the list of resources at the back of the book for some suggestions.) Then take an inventory. This can be an enjoyable task—a bit of sleuth work in the midst of natural paradise. If the identity of a particular tree has you stumped, take a sample leaf to your local cooperative extension office for identification.

Deciding on Your Needs

Next, decide which species you wish to keep. For starters, consider the woodlot's purpose. Is it going to be used strictly as a nature preserve, or will it also share duty as a source for firewood and lumber? Whatever its purpose, the woodlot should contain trees to fit the bill. The inset on page 108 will help you make the best choices.

Firewood

For firewood, hardwoods such as beech, oak, maple, and hickory are your best bet. Quick-growing black locust trees are also a great source of high-heat firewood, and you won't wait a lifetime for a tree to reach harvest height. Elm trees are difficult to split, and the logs don't provide many hot coals. Basswood is much simpler to cut down to size, but you'll have to mix it with other hardwoods if you're depending on the heat. Birch, cherry, apple, and walnut provide the most aromatic scents in the fireplace.

Lumber

A trip to the furniture store will tell you what to keep for lumber. Black walnut, for instance, is a quick grower of impressive stature, and its dark **heartwood**—the central, hardened, nonliving part of the tree—is prized by furniture craftsmen the world over. So valuable are some specimens that they have been illegally harvested by poachers. Cherry, sugar maple, oak, and white ash make valuable lumber. The key is to prune the trees when they're young, so you are left with just one, straight trunk that is free of knots.

Recreation

If you're going to use your woodlots for nature hikes or cross-country skiing, encourage trees that add color or interest. Figure on sugar and red maple; white, red, and scarlet oak; white ash; sweet gum; black tupelo; and hickory for fall splendor. A mix of white and river birch, beech, and hemlock add winter color. Springtime highlights black locust, horse chestnut, Norway maple, linden, dogwood, magnolia, and cherry and other fruit trees. And don't

overlook shrubs and small trees, particularly rhododendron, azalea, and sourwood for shady sites with acid soils
and forsythia, burning bush, hawthorn, Eastern redbud,
and sassafras for border areas.

Fruits and Nuts

To attract wildlife in the woodlands, plant as many fruit-
and nut-bearing species as possible, particularly white
oak, butternut, black cherry, and thornapple. While you're
feeding the birds and animals, don't forget your own
kitchen. Shagbark hickory, pecan, butternut, black walnut,
and American and Chinese chestnut provide tasty morsels
for the side tray. You can also load up on a bountiful
harvest from berry bushes and fruit trees of every descrip-
tion, including sour cherry. Make Indian lemonade from
staghorn sumac, tea from sassafras, and ersatz coffee from
the Kentucky coffeetree. **Caution:** Leave the horse chestnut
behind. The horse chestnut, which is a buckeye and not a
true chestnut, has poisonous nuts.

Stocking the Woodlot

If you want to help nature stock the woodlot, consider
growing some species from seed. It's quite easy to grow
the most common types of trees. All you need are some
empty milk cartons, potting soil, and seeds. Check the
source list at the back of the book for guides on growing
trees and shrubs, or ask the cooperative extension office or
the horticulture department of a nearby college. Some
species, like locust, will germinate freely if you breech the
seed coating before planting. Many deciduous tree seeds
must be **stratified** (put in cold storage) for 2 to 3 months

Good Selections for the Woodlot

After you decide on the function your woodlot will have, choose the trees that satisfy your needs.

LUMBER

Black cherry
Cedar
Black walnut
Red oak
Red pine
Sugar maple
White pine
White ash
White oak

FIREWOOD

Apple
Ash
Beech
Birch
Hickory
Locust
Maple
Oak
Pear

ORNAMENTAL

Aspen
Balsam fir
Chokecherry
Dogwood
Hemlock
Magnolia
Pin oak
Sassafras
Sugar maple
White birch

WET-SITES

Alder
American holly
American arborvitae
Baldcypress
Black tupelo
Dogwood
Larch
Paper birch
Pin oak
Red maple
River birch
Swamp white oak
Sweet gum
Sweet bay magnolia
White spruce
Willow

A Few Easy Trees to Propagate

AMERICAN CHESTNUT *(Castanea dentata)*

The seeds of this tree and those of other true chestnuts will dry out quickly, so keep the nuts cool and moist at all times. Stratify the nuts for 4 months. Then cut a slit in the outer hull. To prevent theft by rodents, try the following trick. Poke holes in the sides of a beer or soda pop can; then cut the bottom out. Drop the nut into the inverted can, pack it with soil, and bury the can right side up so the nut is about an inch below the soil surface. The nut can germinate, the roots can grow, but the squirrels can't get a free meal!

BLACK LOCUST *(Robinia pseudoacacia)*

This tree is the easiest plant to propagate aside from dandelions. The small seeds are contained in pea-like pods that hang from the trees throughout the winter. Because the seeds have an impermeable outer shell, they can be stored for years without losing their viability. When you are ready to start your project, pour boiling water over the seeds for 1 to 3 seconds. Then plant them. They will germinate in about a week, and you won't believe the rapid rate of growth. Thorns quickly develop on young seedlings to keep rodents away.

HORSE CHESTNUT *(Aesculus hippocastanum)*

Don't let the common name fool you: The horse chestnut is a buckeye, not a true chestnut. You cannot eat the nuts, but you can plant them. They germinate so freely that seedlings will emerge in great numbers from nuts that have been raked into a pile with leaf debris. The horse chestnut is a rapid grower with showy white flowers in the late spring. Leaf scorch—the browning of leaves—can be an unsightly problem during the summer.

RED OAK *(Quercus rubra)* AND BLACK OAK *(Quercus velutina)*

Both trees have bitter acorns, so squirrels leave many of them where they drop. However, if you wait till spring to gather the nuts, many will have been lost to weevils that bore into the acorn and destroy the embryo. It's better to gather the nuts in the fall. Soak them in 120-degree water for 30 minutes. Then stratify the acorns for 4 months: Put them in a seal-top plastic bag along with a slightly damp sponge or paper towel, and place the packet in a refrigerator crisper. In the spring, plant the acorns in moist soil and stake the perimeter with chicken wire or another barrier to keep critters at bay.

WHITE OAK *(Quercus alba)*

The acorns of this tree are not as bitter as those of red and black oak, so squirrels gather them without delay. White oak acorns do not need to be stratified. If you plant them indoors in November, they will sprout in December. Left outside, the acorns send out a taproot in the fall. They then lie dormant until spring, when seedlings emerge. As with all oaks, protection of the acorn and seedling from rodents is critical. We recommend loosely wrapping the lower surface of the seedlings with tinfoil and then surrounding the whole plant with a 2-liter plastic bottle that has had the top and bottom cut off.

before they'll germinate. And still others, such as the holly, can take up to 2 years before they sprout. So don't lose hope. (See the inset on page 109 for a discussion of some trees that are easy to propagate.)

Another possibility, especially for those who don't have the patience or time to wait for a seedling to develop, is to visit the garden center midway through the growing season. They'll probably have a number of shrubs and trees on sale, and some places will negotiate on the price if you buy in quantity. Discount stores will also deal in plants, particularly those that aren't looking quite up to snuff. Usually, these plants will bounce right back with some care. (For a step-by-step guide to planting trees and shrubs, see the inset on page 112.)

Choosing Healthy Plants

No matter what the price, though, avoid any evergreens that won't hold their needles or deciduous trees that aren't green under the bark. Use your thumbnail to scratch the surface.

When choosing a nursery plant, don't go for the biggest or the smallest of the lot; try to find a medium-sized specimen. Be wary of any plant with severely wilted or yellowed foliage, as well as plants with cracked or torn bark.

If you do buy a sick plant and put it in your woodlot, leave it in the ground for at least one growing season, even if it looks dead. Healthy young sucker shoots may emerge to save the plant. Keep it watered and give it a boost of phosphorous to encourage root growth.

An acid-loving tree benefits from a top dressing of sawdust and composted manure; the sawdust acidifies the soil while the manure replaces the nitrogen that the saw-

How to Plant Trees and Shrubs

Planting a tree or shrub is a bit like painting a house. On the surface, it's not very complicated. But if you don't do it right—or if you take too many shortcuts—your chances for success are limited.

STEP 1: CONSIDER THE PLANT PACKAGING

Plants are packaged for sale in different ways. Nurseries sell trees and shrubs in three different forms.

- *Container-grown. These plants are easy to handle and transport and have well-developed roots. Unfortunately, these roots can become tangled when a plant is left in the container too long. Tangled roots aren't very good at anchoring a tree.*
- *Balled-and-burlapped (B&B). This form is preferred for handling large specimens (with a caliper of 2 inches or more) and deciduous plants that have leafed out. B&B stock is also easier to plant, since the burlap can be left in place. The downside is that B&B plants are heavier, more expensive, and harder to handle.*
- *Bare-root. These plants are the cheapest of the three. They're also the easiest to handle, making them a natural for mail-order nurseries. Bare-root plants are slower to establish themselves, though, and the roots are prone to damage and drying out.*

STEP 2: STORE THE PLANT

Protecting your tree or shrub before it's planted is a vital, yet often overlooked, step. When transporting, cover the canopy with a canvas tarp to keep wind from drying the foliage. Plastic can be used, but not for extended periods, since heat can build up and damage the plant.

Finding safe, temporary storage is critical, especially with bare-root stock. Unless the humidity is 90 percent or better, a plant will lose moisture for as long as it is out of the ground. To offset that loss, put bare-root stock in a bucket of water for a few hours before "heeling it in" as follows: Select a shady spot, dig a shallow trench, position the plant at a 45-degree angle, and then bury the roots. Keep the plant watered until it is ready for its permanent home. Container-grown and B&B plants also need to be kept cool and out of hot sun.

STEP 3: PREPARE THE SITE

Make sure the final site you've chosen is suitable for the plant. A little homework now will save you a lot of grief down the road. Do the soil conditions meet the plant's requirements? Or is the soil too wet, dry, or acidic? Consider the plant's tolerance for sun, wind, and road salt. Naturally, you'll want to keep trees away from buildings, sewers, septic systems, and utility lines.

When planting, dig a hole that is 50 percent wider than the root ball, but no deeper. Otherwise, the plant will eventually settle deeper than it should. Dig straight down to avoid cone-shaped holes. Position the plant so its best side is highlighted. In very windy areas, you might want to slant trees slightly into the prevailing wind.

STEP 4: PLANT THE TREE OR SHRUB

Once the plant is positioned, fill the hole about halfway with soil. If your soil is sandy, add about 25 percent peat moss to help hold moisture. If the soil is heavy with clay, mix in some peat moss to foster drainage. Fill the hole with water to help settle the soil. Shovel in the remaining soil, and tamp down to remove air pockets, being careful not to bury low branches. In wet areas, mound the soil to encourage runoff. Otherwise, leave a shallow saucer to collect water.

STEP 5: STAKE AND WRAP THE PLANT

In windy areas, trees more than 10 feet tall should be staked temporarily. Fasten three guy wires to stakes radiating from the trunk; then loop each wire around the trunk and back to a stake. Use a section of pliable garden hose to protect the bark of the tree from the wire. Keep the wires taut to prevent the tree from shaking and the roots from loosening. Remove the stakes in a year, before the wires have a chance to girdle the tree.

While some horticulturists oppose wrapping trees and shrubs, wrapping can be a good idea in some cases. A protective wrap keeps rodents and deer from damaging the bark and can prevent sun scald and frost cracking. Since paper and burlap wraps can cause a moisture problem and become a home to insects, it's better to use plastic tree guards or fine wire mesh, unless you're prepared to remove the paper or burlap wrap each spring and replace it in the fall.

STEP 6: PRUNE THE FOLIAGE

When working with bare-root plants, prune the foliage to create a 3 to 1 ratio of shoots to roots. Since the roots must feed the plant, it's best to lessen their burden whenever possible. The appropriate time for pruning depends on both species and growing region, but don't go much past October 1, since plants need to begin their healing process before winter. Damaged or diseased branches can be trimmed any time, however.

STEP 7: WATER THE PLANT

Water throughout the growing season. Most plants can use at least an inch of water per week, in addition to rainfall. It's best to soak the ground once a week rather than sprinkle daily. Soaking allows water to penetrate more deeply into the soil, and it encourages downward root growth.

STEP 8: FERTILIZE THE SITE

Adding a handful of bonemeal at planting time will encourage root growth because of the high amount of phosphorus. Wood ashes are good, too, since the potassium helps plants suppress diseases and become winter hardy. Be aware that wood ashes can lower the soil acidity, much to the chagrin of acid-loving plants such as oak, pine, and rhododendron.

Don't add manure or anything else high in nitrogen to a new shrub or tree because it will encourage the growth of foliage. Wait until the plant is firmly established. Remember: You can do more damage by fertilizing than by not fertilizing. Most plants can fend for themselves.

---

dust uses to decompose. Pine needles and coffee grounds are fine, too. For plants that prefer a sweeter soil, use wood ashes instead.

Tending the Ground

One of the best things about a woodlot is that you don't have to rake leaves in the fall. That's not only good for you, it's good for the trees. Forest soil contains many beneficial microorganisms that keep soil-borne plant pathogens in check. These beneficial microorganisms—the "good guys"—often are absent from the sterile subsoil brought to the surface of new homesites. Older landscapes can suffer the problem, too, since the soil is usually covered with grass and is not being replenished by decomposing organic matter. In either situation, trees are less able to fend off diseases, especially when they're under stress. Maples and butternuts, for instance, usually develop more problems in a domestic landscape than in a forest setting, and that is directly related to the quality of the soil.

Although woodlots have their share of natural debris—leaves, branches, dead trees—properly managed groves will keep the buildup to a minimum and lessen the chance of fire. Leaves and sticks are fine. They not only give the soil a boost, as we have seen, they also retain moisture and minimize weeds. It's best to leave them right where they are.

While sticks and leaves are good for your trees, you'll probably want to remove large piles of brush. Cut the larger branches into kindling for the fireplace or campfire. Hickory, sugar maple, and white oak branches can be cut into small pieces and added to the barbecue to give a smoky flavor. Black locust, cedar, and chestnut, when you find the rare one, can be made into long-lasting fence posts and landscape timbers superior to pressure-treated wood in resistance to rot.

Smaller branches from any kind of tree can be cut into garden stakes or made into wood chips. While many people like to use wood chips around foundation plantings in their yard, we think a better idea is to spread them along walking paths. If you do put wood chips around plants in the garden, make sure they are seasoned. Otherwise they'll suck nitrogen out of the soil as they decompose. Wood chips from evergreens are preferable to those of hardwoods, since they are sappier and thus less likely to contain diseases and pests.

Harvesting and Pruning Trees

Woodlands are home to many insects and fungi, both beneficial and harmful. As with other plant life, trees that are healthy and vigorous are less likely to be attacked by insects and disease-causing fungi. Providing adequate growing space and removing weak and diseased trees will do much to prevent a malady of epidemic proportions. Unfortunately, many who harvest woodlands go straight to the healthier trees, allowing the weak and diseased trees to remain. This not only allows diseases to spread, it also encourages survival of the weakest. Nature never planned it that way.

At harvest time, remove weak and diseased trees. Signs of weakness and decay include woodpecker holes and growth of mold and lichen. When you find a diseased tree, dispose of it quickly, preferably by burning. If you're removing only part of the tree—a limb or some branches— apply some bleach to the saw blade before each cut to lessen the chance of spreading the disease to different parts of the tree. A spray bottle is good for this task.

While you're pruning, be on the lookout for damaged wood, which can weaken the tree, as well as irregularities—top-heavy branches, V-shaped crotches, or multiple stems. These characteristics are undesirable because they make trees more susceptible to damage from wind, rain, or snow. Try to leave one central leader, with branches attached closer to a 90-degree angle than to a 45-degree angle.

In a woodlot, properly spaced trees are self-pruning. Competing for limited sunlight, they develop one primary stem and lose lower branches. But trees growing too far apart have large, knot-producing branches almost to the ground; their trunks taper from bottom to top and are usually forked or crooked. They're fine as specimen trees in the landscape, but ill-conceived for the properly managed woodlot. The same goes for the trees growing too close together. Deprived of sufficient sunlight, water, and minerals for growth, they are small and spindly for their age. The prescription is to thin the ranks, lessening the competition but not eliminating it entirely.

A well-managed woodlot, whether it be a pine grove or hardwood forest, is a joy to behold—nature at its finest. Many hours of enjoyment can be had not only in visiting a woodlot but also in taking care of it. As the old expression goes, getting there is half the fun.

Glossary

auger. A tool used for boring holes in soil.

biodynamics. A theory of agriculture that emphasizes the natural relationships among plants, and between plants and the soil and other natural elements.

companion planting. The strategic arrangement of crops to keep away insects and otherwise improve the health of plants.

compost. Any organic matter that has been allowed to decay into humus so that it can be used for fertilizing and enriching soil.

cover crop. A crop planted to improve the soil and not meant to be harvested.

dieback. A condition in which the peripheral parts of woody plants die.

disk. To slice through soil repeatedly with an implement.

dolomite. Calcium magnesium carbonate. Used to lower the acidity of soil.

green manure. A crop that is planted specifically to be plowed under.

hardpan. A compacted, often clayey layer of soil that it is nearly impossible for roots to penetrate.

heartwood. The central, hardened, nonliving part of the treetrunk.

humates. Deposits of mineralized organic matter formed in much the same way as coal.

humus. Partially decomposed organic matter rich in nutrients.

mulch. Any substance, including plastic tarp, that covers the ground around plants and between rows.

nematodes. Microscopic parasites that live in soil.

pH. A numerical measure of acidity, with 7 being neutral. Lower numbers indicate increasing acidity, and higher numbers, increasing alkalinity (that is, decreasing acidity).

phosphate. A phosphorus compound used as a fertilizer.

potash. A potassium compound—potassium chloride—used as a fertilizer.

stratify. To put seeds in cold storage, necessary for germination.

tilth. Cultivation of soil.

topsoil. The layer of soil which is richest in organic material and in which plants generally have their roots.

Selected Readings

Abraham, Doc and Katy. *Green Thumb Wisdom.* Pownal, Vermont: Storey Communications, Inc. (Schoolhouse Road, Pownal, VT 05261), 1996.

Common Weeds of the United States. Based on material by the Agricultural Research Service, U.S.D.A. New York: Dover Publications, Inc. (180 Varick Street, New York, NY 10014), 1970.

Degraaf, R. M., and G. M. Witman. *Trees, Shrubs, and Vines for Attracting Birds.* Amherst: Univ. of Mass. Press, 1979.

Dirr, Michael. *A Manual of Woody Landscape Plants.* Chicago: Stipes Publishing (10-12 Chester Street, Chicago, IL 61820), 1990.

Imes, Rick. *The Practical Botanist.* New York: Simon & Schuster, Inc., 1982.

Rodale, J. I. *The Encyclopedia of Organic Gardening.* Emmaus, Penn.: Rodale Books, Inc., 1971.

Sources of Propagated Native Plants and Wildflowers. Framingham, Mass.: New England Wildflower Society (180 Hemenway Road, Framingham, MA 01701), 1995.

U.S. Forest Service. *Seeds of Woody Plants in the United States* U.S.D.A. Handbook No. 450. Washington, D.C.: U.S. Government Printing Office, 1974.

Wyman, Donald. *Trees for American Gardens.* New York: Macmillan, 1990.

Index

B

C

F

G

H